THE SAS GUIDE TO TRACKING

THE SAS
GUIDE TO TRACKING

Bob Carss

with

Stewart Birch

Illustrations by Roy Thomasson

THE LYONS PRESS

To Ben Carss

Printed in Canada

10 9 8 7 6 5 4 3 2 1

First published in Great Britain 1999 by Charles
Constable & Company, Ltd.

First Lyons Press edition, 2000

Library of Congress Cataloging-in-Publication Data

Carss, Bob.

The SAS guide to tracking / Bob Carss with Stewart Birch;
    illustrations by Roy Thomasson.
        p. cm.
    Includes index.
    ISBN 1-58574-031-4 (pb.)
    1. Tracking and trailing. 2. Animal Tracks. 3. Footprints. I. Title.

SK282.C37   2000
599.147'9 21
                                                                99-087699
                                                                CIP

'It happened one day, about noon, going towards my boat, I was exceedingly surprised with the print of a man's naked foot on the shore, which was very plain to be seen in the sand . . .'

Daniel Defoe, *Robinson Crusoe*

Contents

Part Three: Advanced skills

Part Four: The Future

List of Illustrations

Acknowledgments

In the first instance my debt of gratitude is to 22 Special Air Service Regiment and the New Zealand Special Air Service and all their highly talented jungle instructors who taught me tracking and, most importantly, introduced me to the Iban trackers of Brunei from whom I was able to learn a great deal by observing their methods.

Also I would like to thank Roy Thomasson, not only for his illustrations which breathe life into the subject matter, but also for his support throughout this enterprise especially in the early stages when his encouragement sustained me. Thanks are also due to Stewart Birch for his help in editing and writing the guide.

Metric Conversions

The measurements in this book are given in metric units. The following table is provided as a reference for conversion to corresponding U.S. weights and measures.

Length

1 m = 39.4 in	= 3.28 ft	1 ft = 12 in = 0.305 m
1 km = 0.62 miles	= 3274 ft	1 mile = 5280 ft = 1.61 km

Area

1 sq km   = .386 sq miles   1 sq mile = 2.59 sq km
1 hectare = 2.47 acres   1 acre   = 0.405 hectares

Mass

1 kg = 2.21 pounds   1 pound = .452 kg
1 g = .035 ounces   1 ounce = 28.6 g

Capacity

1 liter = 1.057 qt = 0.264 gallons   1 gallon = 4 qt = 3.78 liter

Introduction

This book is about tracking – a serious subject in which I am passionately involved. It is not about the SAS. I was fortunate enough to have served in the SAS for eighteen years and whilst there enhanced and developed my interest in tracking – that is the connection. Don't expect to find any state secrets in this book. The only secrets that I wish to pass on are those from nature which are gained by the study and practice of the art of tracking. I hope this study will enrich your lives as much as it has enriched mine.

I was born in the urban environment of Newcastle. My mother and father moved when I was very young and I was brought up in Kelso, a small market town on the English/Scottish border. This was to be the start of my interest in country life and nature. I learnt a lot from going fishing and walking with my father, listening to and watching local people and from the many days spent wandering the countryside as a young boy.

By the age of fifteen I knew a great deal about the countryside and the wild life it supported, and had learnt some valuable lessons. These were to become useful to me throughout my military career. I left Kelso when I was fifteen years of age and joined the Army as a boy soldier. I enlisted as Junior Private Carss in the 1st Battalion of the King's Own Scottish Borderers (KOSB's) at Pennycuik barracks near Edinburgh. I felt immensely proud being able to join this infantry regiment. At seventeen and a half, after my 'apprenticeship', I was posted to my battalion in Germany. I later served with them in a number of overseas postings. I enjoyed life in the KOSB's, but by 1971 I felt the need for a greater challenge so I applied for and passed selection for the SAS which is based in Hereford – the city which has been my home ever since.

My service in the SAS took me all over the world and the work was always varied and interesting. All volunteers for the SAS have to undergo jungle training which forms an important part of the selection and continuation training. My jungle training was conducted by the very experienced Regimental Sergeant Major (RSM), 'Geordie' Tindale and was immediately followed by a tracking course run by very able and enthusiastic NCOs who shared a passionate interest in tracking and jungle soldiering. Learning to track with very knowledgeable and very experienced men – men who had spent years on operations throughout the world brought to life all the things I had learned as a child roaming the countryside. It was hard work, but it suited me down to the ground and this early period in the SAS was a deeply satisfying time for me.

The SAS, like any sound organisation, tries to match the allocation of jobs to people's interests and abilities, so I was often sent to work in jungle environments. Eventually I spent several years teaching others the art of tracking and how to live and work in the jungle.

Now that I am back in civilian life I have continued taking an active interest in the outdoor, country life. I feel that there is a great deal that I would like to pass onto others. I look forward to the day when I can go out into the countryside with my young son, Ben, to whom this book is dedicated, and pass onto him my enthusiasm for the natural world.

The SAS Guide to Tracking is a book that is designed to appeal to all ages from all backgrounds, and the use of the male pronouns should be read as meaning both genders. It draws heavily upon my personal experience and my military career – especially my practical knowledge of the countryside. Although superficially certain chapters are of more significance to specialist groups, I recommend all readers to sample all the chapters – there is much to be learnt from a cross-fertilisation of ideas in tracking as in many inter-disciplinary subjects. The outdoor pursuits teacher will learn from the jungle experiences of a soldier, just as much as an NCO instructor will profit from the lateral thinking of the psychologist.

The book starts by putting tracking into a modern perspective by briefly looking at its development and then showing the present day applications. After describing the type of personality the tracker is trying to foster, we then have a foundation chapter which defines the tracking terms. From this base line the book progresses through a study of sign to the development of the powers of observation, movement (stalking), into the track pursuit drill proper. Once the principles of the drill are established, we move onto specific examples with chapters dedicated to advanced techniques. And finally, you will find three or four pages for you to record your own notes. Although you may wish to use a note book, I thought it necessary to make the point that you never stop learning about tracking – you will learn new lessons from each follow.

This book will guide you stage by stage through the various practices which lead up to tracking itself.

If you are prepared to put the skills into practice as you read through the book, you will start to assimilate the knowledge straight away. By the end of the book you will be well on the road to starting your career as a tracker.

To be a successful tracker, as in any other occupation, you will have to adhere to the age old adage that nothing is achieved except by hard, conscientious work.

Read the book!
Follow the spoor!
Good luck!

PART ONE

The Briefing

CHAPTER ONE

Tracking Today – Some Modern Applications

People's first comment, or at least their first thoughts, when they hear an account of an incident where tracking has been employed is something along the lines of, 'How unusual!' It is as if they thought the type of skills associated with trackers and tracking had died out long ago, and the disciplines had no relevance to modern day life. My aim is to dispel this misconception and to open up the benefits of tracking to a much wider audience. At the moment there are, it seems, only two groups who are aware of the usefulness of the tracker's knowledge in modern society.

Firstly, there are the specialist military units who have kept the skills alive – despite great resistance from some quarters of the military establishment. And secondly, there are the rural police forces who have brought in trackers, usually ex-military, on a case by case basis but who rarely have a formal training programme for their own trackers.

In my opinion this is a sad under-utilisation of a wealth of knowledge that our ancestors have built up over the millennia and I believe that tracking can play a wider and valuable role in modern society.

A HISTORICAL PERSPECTIVE

The development of the skill was initially brought about by man's desire for meat. Because he was naturally weaker than most of his prey and his weapons were primitive he was forced to use other skills. He had to observe the areas frequented by and the habitats of the animals and birds which he intended catching for food.

This basic feature is reflected even today in that some of the best game trackers in the world come from the more remote areas where they live a very unsophisticated existence close to nature. Often their way of life, customs and social habits are dominated by the 'game chase' and the 'after catch' celebrations. A classic example of this hunting-centred lifestyle were the Great Plains Indians of North America. They migrated with the game herds which not only provided them with food, but also clothing, ornaments, tools, shelter and fuel. It is not surprising that their dances and their spiritual life were fashioned around the buffalo and the other animals which supported them. This is just one example of how fundamental hunting and therefore tracking is to mankind.

Even after man had domesticated animals and cultivated the land tracking did not become redundant. It was a skill in his arsenal when warring against other tribes. He soon found that even with inferior numbers and weapons, by employing stealth, cunning, surprise, and superior knowledge of bush craft he was able to overcome and defeat his victims. Reprisals and revenge naturally followed, and so tracking and scouting skills were firmly established in warfare.

The vast majority of the civilian population and even military leaders and police chiefs are unaware of the potential use of trained trackers, but, with some imagination, it is not difficult to envisage its many uses.

LAW ENFORCEMENT AGENCIES

Tracking with most law enforcement agencies is orientated primarily towards scent tracking, employing highly trained tracker dogs. Their work ranges from the pursuit of law-breaking fugitives to the detection of explosives and narcotics. The USA border patrol is but one enforcement agency which currently employs these tracking techniques in its never-ending task of stopping illegal entry into the USA.

Scent tracking is established as a useful tool but the same enthusiasm has not yet extended to the visual tracker whose expertise could equally well be used. To limit the use of tracking to scent tracking is to impose a severe limitation. The visual tracker would be especially useful in rural areas.

In my opinion there are two areas in which visual trackers should be involved with police work. Firstly, there should be a pool of Home Office-certified trackers who are on call to constabularies – rather like interpreters are on call. And secondly, they have a briefing role – to explain to senior officers the applications of visual tracking and to make all officers aware of the importance of preserving the sign (see Chapter Two) for the tracker.

THE MILITARY

Military tracking in the second half of the twentieth century provides many examples of the application of this ancient skill. It is man tracking man, either to gain information or to kill him. The low-intensity, counter-insurgency wars of the post-colonial era provide many examples of the employment of trackers. It is such a rich and varied field that I have devoted a whole chapter to it – see Chapter Eighteen. But even here, once the conflicts have been resolved, the tracking units are usually disbanded and the men remustered, thus dispersing and eventually losing the pool of skills. The New Zealand SAS is one unit which has had the foresight to keep tracking skills as an essential component of the military curriculum.

The benefits of preserving the knowledge and skills of a tracker within a military establishment are twofold. Firstly, the training which a tracker undergoes can be seen as honing the already necessary skills which any infantry soldier needs – observation, movement and concealment. And secondly, the skills are ready for immediate utilisation by the higher commands in such bushfire emergency situations as search and rescue of downed pilots, as in Iraq or Bosnia, when the TACBE (the emergency beacon carried by aircrew for locating purposes) may have been lost, damaged, have run out of power, been stolen or removed if the aircrew have been captured.

CAVE AND MOUNTAIN RESCUE

These organisations are often called upon to locate missing persons. Unfortunately, they possess limited or no knowledge in the arts of tracking. Consequently a great deal of sign (see Chapter Two) is normally obliterated by the first person on the scene, making it almost impossible for any immediate pursuit by trained trackers. Vital time is wasted and the results can be tragic.

CONSERVATIONISTS

For the nature enthusiast, whether he is a professional paid conservation officer or the unpaid amateur working for the RSPB, there is a great benefit to be had from a proper grounding in tracking. With a fuller understanding of what is happening in their particular environment they gain a greater satisfaction from their pursuits, and professionals are better placed to protect species and encourage the development of the wildlife.

GAMEKEEPERS

As any professional gamekeeper knows, he is now protecting a very valuable asset for his employer. Land and livestock are under threat from ruthless, well-organised gangs, both locally raised and, perhaps more importantly, from out of area. These criminals do not enter a region on a whim. They plan their raids with precision because they know the profits to be gained from their enterprises are huge. The knowledge that a trained tracker could elicit from studying the areas where either raids have taken place or, even better, where the reconnaisance and preparation for a raid has taken place, would be an invaluable weapon in the anti-poaching units' armoury. This is not just of relevance to the African government trying to protect its stock of rhino but also to the Yorkshire or Scottish gamekeeper trying to preserve his stocks of pheasants and salmon.

A gamekeeper's use of tracking skills is not confined to anti-poaching activities, they can also be used in order to protect their charges from other wildlife predators. To catch, trap, shoot or control the wild life in their area of operation they must first be able to locate and identify the areas frequented by these animals.

FARMERS AND LIVESTOCK OWNERS

The activities of rustlers may conjure up romantic images of the Wild West but to the Welsh sheep farmer or the private zoo-owner who has a rare species stolen it is simply a matter of common-or-garden theft. Often though, the environment in which these crimes take place is ideally suited to the effective deployment of a tracker – if the owners are aware and do not foul the sign.

COUNTRY RECREATIONALISTS

Any person who is interested in the countryside is only seeing a fraction of the life around him if he hasn't got the tracker's awareness of the observation of detail. This knowledge can enhance a country-based hobby beyond belief. It is the difference between an illiterate and a literate person standing in front of a signpost. Orienteers, fell walkers, fishermen, hunters, botanists, and anyone with a love of or an interest in nature will find that their enjoyment and knowledge increases tremendously.

THE EDUCATIONALIST

For the adult who has responsibilities for the personal development of the young and for the educationalist in general there is profound value in the study of tracking. It may seem paradoxical that a topic so readily associated with warlike activities should be proposed as being of use to the teacher in a liberal democracy but I'm sure the following observations will banish any preconceived ideas.

Observation, memory, analysis, and deduction are all fundamental mental operations which need to be cultivated in the young mind – they happen to be the basis of the tracker's mental process. So what better way to develop these processes than in an educationally fun environment for groups of all ages. I see this being extremely efficacious with children who have not responded well in a more formal teaching setting, or as an adjunct and enforcement in an outdoor pursuits environment. As well as developing the rational skills, the emotional traits inculcated by tracker training are also of great worth – patience, determination, concentration, and an appreciation and respect for the countryside and its wildlife (see Chapter Five for a full exposition of the qualities of a tracker and Chapter Seventeen for the material which is specifically for the teacher and instructor). The educational value of tracking should not be underestimated and there is a good argument for introducing tracking into any outdoor pursuits' syllabus in schools. One can see the development of a tracker as a progress through several stages. First of all he must cultivate his powers of observation and attention to detail. Then he must develop and practise his memory and deduction. Along with these skills other habits of perseverance and patience are being encouraged.

I am sure that many in the armed forces, the police, the cave and mountain rescue services will find invaluable, and possibly lifesaving, lessons in this book. For other groups such as conservationists, ornithologists, and country sportsmen and women the knowledge contained in this book will enhance their understanding and enjoyment of their pastimes.

And finally, for the young person, I hope this book fosters an interest in the countryside, conservation and nature, just as the following incident did for me when I was lucky enough to have it explained to me by the gamekeeper. We were out walking one winter's morning when he pointed out where a rabbit had been crouching in the snow – there was a round patch about five by nine inches. Then he showed me how the rabbit must have been startled as it accelerated suddenly – the hind feet were ahead of the fore feet within a few paces. Then the rabbit's path became erratic. It was trying to escape but there were no other tracks. Then he showed me a few spots of blood. The rabbit had been attacked but by a hunter that left no track. To a six-year-old this was a mystery – obvious when the gamekeeper told me about hawks and owls. We then found a great deal more blood. And then the remains of the rabbit. The gamekeeper showed me the prints of the bird of prey in the snow by the rabbit's carcass. He was just about to outline in the snow the difference between a hawk's print and that of an owl's when the rabbit's attacker came swooping in to finish its meal and prove the gamekeeper right. The sort of incident you never forget!

CHAPTER TWO

Some Definitions and Explanations

Before going any further I would like to mention some of the terms used in tracking that you will find useful throughout this book. They are organised in like groups and so that the earlier ones will help to explain the later entries.

TRACKING
Tracking can be defined as the art of being able to locate, identify and pursue sign and, from intelligent interpretations and deductions, gain reasonably accurate information about the quarry concerned. The same skills apply whether it is a human being, an animal, a bird, or a vehicle. When applied to animals, in particular, it has been known by different names in different continents – trailing in North America, spooring in Africa, and pugging in India. Put simply, tracking is the following and interpretation of sign.

SIGN
This is any physical indication which is left, on or in the environment, by the passage of any animal or inanimate object. The following are some examples of visual signs:
- Sap from a bruised root or trunk of a tree
- Disturbance to animal, bird or insect life
- Change in colour and unnatural formation of vegetation due to disturbance
- Lack of water and dew on vegetation
- Footprints in bare or muddy ground
- Mud, soil or sand on vegetation
- Animal droppings, fur, feathers, and bones
- Bruises, breaks and cuts in vegetation

GROUND SIGN
These are ground-level marks or disturbances. (See also Chapter Three.)

TOP SIGN

This is defined as any sign above the ankle. (See also Chapter Three.)

CONCLUSIVE SIGN

This is sign which is directly linked to the quarry, such as a boot print in soft ground. (See also Chapter Three.)

SUBSTANTIATING SIGN

This is sign which has probably been made by the quarry but it cannot be tied to him conclusively. (See also Chapter Three.)

KEY SIGN

This is the sign which is the most prominent. The track may have twenty to thirty different types of sign and the tracker will have to be familiar with all these. But, in fact, he will be concentrating on a combination of two to three signs at any one time – these are the key signs. Because of the nature of the ground and changes in vegetation, key signs will change and one will become more important than another at any one time. The key sign will vary depending on the landscape, be it primary and secondary forest, scrub, swamp and grassland, or desert and snow-covered areas. Obviously some signs are common to all areas, such as a footprint or a tyre track. Key sign, like all sign, is affected by climatic and seasonal changes. It alters with the time of day and before, during and after snow or rain – all of which will greatly influence the amount of sign left in any area.

SIGN PATTERN

This is the sign that serves to indicate the habits or the peculiarities of a quarry. This information may be of a particular individual or it may be building up a profile of the group or species. An example of this would be deer coming out of the forests at dusk to graze on the farmer's crops.

TIME BRACKET

All sign in the initial stages is placed into a time bracket, this is, the time lapse between the earliest possible time that the sign could have been made and the time it was located.

STRAIGHT EDGE

This is the line found on leaves or blades of grass caused by the application of pressure. Most leaves, dry or green, are curled and if trodden on will break or bend in a straight line. Usually dry leaves will break and green or wet leaves will bend. From the straight edges on the leaves, see figure 1, we can tell the approximate size of the footprint which, in turn, will help us to determine the size of the quarry. This can be demonstrated by treading on a small cardboard cylinder, such as a toilet paper roll (see figure 2), which creates two straight edges. The width of your shoe would be shown by the distance between the 'straight edges'.

Figure 1   Examples of straight edges on vegetation

SPOOR

This word derives from the Dutch word for footprint and is reserved for that sign which is left by an animal (including man), as opposed to the sign left by a vehicle or inanimate object.

THE TRACK

This is the line of sign. The derivation of the word 'track' is uncertain but it is generally thought that the original sense described the line or mark made on the ground by anything

Figure 2   Straight edges and their relationship to the size of
the footwear

hauled or dragged. Now the meaning of the word extends to
include the mark, or series of marks, or any physical indication
left by the passage of anything – a wheel, the wake of a ship, a
series of footprints, animal spoor, scent, any residual heat and
even microscopically recognised material in genetic tracking.

VISUAL TRACKING

This is the art of being able to track a human being, animal, or
vehicle, by the marks it has left. It should be remembered that it
is difficult for anything to move in an environment without
leaving some sign which is noticeable to the trained eye. A visual
tracker relies primarily on sight and is therefore unable to track
by night except in very unusual circumstances such as brilliant
moonlight, bright ambient light, with the use of a torch, or by
using night viewing devices such as goggles or scopes.

SCENT TRACKING

Scent tracking is normally performed by dogs. However, a well-
trained visual tracker can follow a quarry, either human or
animal, by its scent – the scent needs to be strong and fresh. In

addition the visual tracker may be alerted to potential dangers by detecting smells such as:

- Cooking odours
- Smoke
- Latrines
- Newly dug earth

TRACKING PICTURE

This is the overall picture gained by the tracker over any given length of track. It is like a story to a good tracker. To obtain the complete tracking picture you would have to follow the track until you could state with accuracy the complete details of the quarry being followed. The track picture builds up continuously with each new piece of information gained. An experienced tracker will be able to deduce part of the track picture after following for only a short distance.

TRACKING MEDIUM

This is the generic term used for the material in which the sign was left by the quarry. For example, mud and sand are tracking media which obviously retain sign, whereas rock and water do hold sign but it is far more difficult to detect.

EXIT AND ENTRY POINTS

These are points or passage ways through which a quarry may pass from one environment to another, for example, from a pine wood to a corn field, from a grass field to a road, from a ploughed field back into a wood.

POINTERS

These are the signs that serve to indicate the direction of movement. They can either be ground or top sign – see figure 3 for examples. Low foliage, grass, ferns when trampled on or brushed forward will remain in the direction of the movement until disturbed again. When a person or animal brushes past a small tree a number of leaves may become entangled. These may be seen from a distance after practice. If the base of the tree was tapped the leaves would fall back into their natural position. The leaves or branches will be tangled towards the direction of

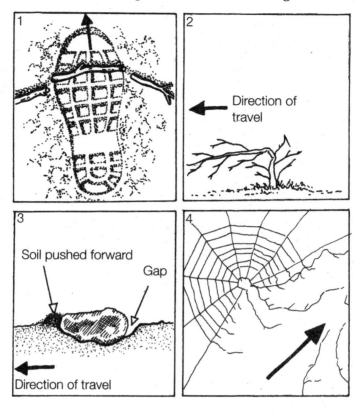

Figure 3   Examples of pointers

movement – these are the pointers. If the ground and top sign pointers contradict each other it is possible that the quarry was walking backwards, that is, the prints on the ground would be facing one way but the evidence from the disturbed foliage would indicate a different direction of travel. On the other hand if the top sign pointers contradict themselves, in the case of a human quarry, then it could be that the sign has been re-arranged. For example, a man using this deception tactic would deliberately bend vegetation in the opposite direction to his line of travel.

FOUL TRACK
Is defined as a track that has entered an area where numerous other tracks exit, for example, at a watering hole, or a feeding area. Figure 4 shows some specific examples of individually fouled prints.

Child's footprint superimposed over that of an adult

Dog's footprint superimposed over that of a pig

Figure 4   Fouled tracks

DECEPTION

If a quarry knows they are being followed they will invariably try to lose the tracker by deception. Unless they are extremely efficient in their deception methods they will more often than not 'sign post' their change of direction – see Indicator Pace below.

INDICATOR PACE

This is the footprint immediately before or after an intended change of direction, see figure 5. The initial indications of this can be seen at the prints marked as 1 and 2, 1 being the indicator pace as it is now pointing, or indicating a possible change of direction. The print marked as 3 gives the first full indication of the new direction of travel. At a walking pace a ninety degree change of direction will normally be indicated by two shorter paces as the turn is executed – in this case between 1 and 2.

CASTING

This is the method of locating or relocating sign that has been lost, or where a tracker is endeavouring to locate a start point at an incident area – see Chapter Sixteen.

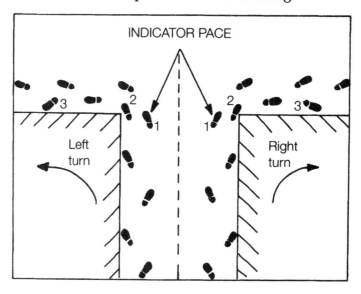

Figure 5   Indicator pace

TUNING IN

This is the initial reading of the sign that enables the tracker to think and act as the quarry. This will assist the tracker to anticipate future actions the quarry may take. The time taken for the tracker to tune into a new environment depends on their tracking ability. To give an illustration, imagine that you have been following a quarry through a wood for three hours and your main 'key signs' were pointers, all of a sudden the quarry's sign exits the wood and goes across a grass field. You will have to reassess the situation, the ground has changed and the 'key sign' will now probably have changed to footprints. It may take you up to half an hour before you feel comfortable in pursuing the quarry's sign – it is in this sort of area that tracking crosses over from being a science to being an art.

PACE TRACKING

This is 'pace for pace' tracking carried out during the 'tuning in' period or when the track becomes difficult to pursue. It will be mainly ground sign that you will be following when pace tracking and you have to start from a known quarry's sign, whether it is conclusive or substantiating sign. Then make a comprehensive study of that particular sign to gain as much information as you can, direction, size of print, width, depth, left or right foot, fore or hind in the case of an animal, sex, and age. Once you have taken all these into consideration, your next task will be to find the next sign and so on.

TRACK ISOLATION

This is where the tracker, having anticipated the intended route, is able to abandon the track and leapfrog ahead. To do this with any guarantee of success you must be able to extrapolate the direction of travel by information from some other source. This technique can be used not only to gain time in the pursuit of a human quarry but, if the sign is getting colder and older, you may have the added bonus of finding fresher sign.

TRAITS

These are the characteristic features or qualities distinguishing a particular quarry, for example:
- a limp
- a missing limb
- a pair of unevenly worn shoes
- a horse with a thrown or damaged shoe

PHYSIQUE

This relates to the general appearance of the quarry.

DIET

This relates to the food and drink that the quarry regularly consumes.

HABITAT

This is where the quarry lives. It can be described as:
- Rural
- Suburban
- City
- Remote – away from any population centre

CHAPTER THREE

Sign in Tracking – Defined and Explained

The term sign as used in visual tracking can be defined as any evidence of change from the natural state that is inflicted upon any one geographical environment by the passage of the quarry, whether it may be man, animal or machinery. All sign is rigidly divided into two categories:

- Top sign – this is above the ankle
- Ground sign – anything below the ankle

TOP SIGN

This is found in vegetation which is above the ankle and the zone extends to the height and to the width of the quarry. As the quarry passes through the undergrowth it brushes past and causes unnatural disturbances to the growing vegetation. In the case of birds this zone can extend to the height limit of the vegetation, while the down draught of aircraft, especially helicopters, can create an enormous amount of top sign.

Some examples of top sign:

- Changes in the colour of vegetation
- Unnatural position of vegetation
- Broken fences, gates and stiles
- Disturbance to animals' and birds' nests
- Cutting of vegetation
- Disarranged cobwebs
- Chewed bark and roots
- Hand holds on trees
- Animal and bird roosting sites quite often marked by droppings
- Bruised moss on trees
- Dew swept from vegetation
- Disturbance to the animal kingdom

- Broken twigs, branches, and leaves
- Man-made objects hanging on trees
- Scratches on trees
- Animal droppings, fur, feathers, and skeletons
- Shadow and shine irregularities on vegetation
- Birds and animals being put to flight
- Animal runs making tunnels through the vegetation or marks up trees

GROUND SIGN

This is the sign left mainly by the quarry's feet. This occurs where vegetation from the ground surface has been disturbed by the quarry passing through and over the area.

Some examples of ground sign are:
- Foot and scuff marks
- Animal droppings, latrines, scrapes, and scent-marking areas
- Animal fur, feathers, skin and skeletons
- Animal homes – rabbit burrows, fox dens, and badger setts
- Animal wallowing/rolling sites
- Bird nests
- Bird nests floating on water
- Bird dusting sites
- Footprints – shoes, hoof, claw, and pad
- Bruised or bleeding roots
- Disturbance to the insect life on the ground
- Disturbance or colour change to the ground vegetation
- Mud, sand, and soil deposited by the quarry – see 'Transfer' below
- Disturbed leaves, stones, sticks, worm casts, mole hills, and pock marks
- Debris dropped beside the tracks – cigarette ends, sweet papers, and soft drink cans
- Debris blowing along the top of snow or sand which leaves marks
- Disturbed water
- Dew swept from vegetation
- Flattening and colour changes in the rest up areas of the quarry

- Feather tip markings where a bird has taken off or landed – best seen in snow or mud
- Bruised, squashed, bent, and broken roots, berries, droppings, leaves or twigs

CHARACTERISTICS OF SIGN

Sign may be identified by one or a combination of the following characteristics:

Regularity   This is an effect caused by straight lines, arches or other geometrical shapes being pressed into the ground leaving marks not normally found in nature, e.g. boot marks, vehicle tyre marks.

Flattening   This is the general levelling or depression caused by pressure on an area compared to the immediate surroundings, e.g. the quarry's resting or sleeping area in grass, sand, or snow.

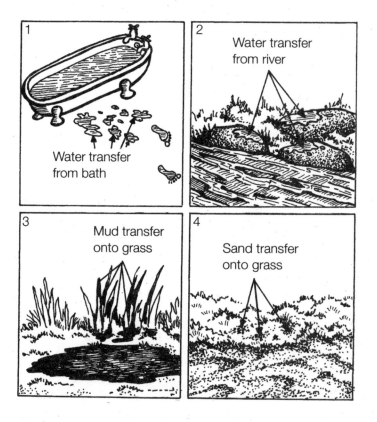

Figure 6   Transfer of sign

Transfer   This is the deposit carried forward over an area after the quarry has moved from one environment to another, e.g. sand, mud, soil, or water which is not in its original position – see figure 6 for some illustrations of the transfer of sign. A couple of everyday examples of transfer are the drops of water left on the bathroom floor when someone steps out of the bath, not the footprint, but the drops that fall from them, and the droplets that fall from your hands as you reach for the hand towel from the washbasin.

Colour change   This is the difference in colour or texture of sign from the area that surrounds it, e.g. overturned droppings, stones, earth, twigs, or leaves will all give a colour change to their immediate surrounding area when disturbed.

Discardables   This is anything that is left behind by the quarry, e.g. fur, feathers, droppings, cigarette ends, sweet papers, tin cans and the remains of food.

Disturbances   This is any other change or rearrangement to the natural state of an area caused by the passage of the quarry, e.g. disturbance of the animal, bird, fish, and insect life, or to water.

CLASSIFICATION OF SIGNS

For tracking purposes we acknowledge four classes of sign:

- Substantiating
- Conclusive
- Temporary
- Permanent

Substantiating sign   These are signs that may or may not have been caused by the quarry. With experience and practice a tracker can, with confidence, class these as conclusive. However, two or more may have to be identified to convince a learner that he is still pursuing the same quarry. Examples are broken twigs, bleeding and bruised roots, broken cobwebs, disturbed water.

Conclusive sign   This class of sign indicates without any more evidence to a tracker the passage of the quarry through the area. This is the sign that has definitely been made by the quarry which you are tracking. Examples are a characteristic footprint, identifiable droppings, a discarded piece of equipment.

Temporary sign   Some types of sign are termed temporary because they are particularly affected by weathering agents such as the wind, rain, snow, and the sun – see Chapter Four for a full description. This is the unavoidable sign left during and after the quarry has passed through an environment, however careful he is. These signs will eventually settle down and return to normal after a lapse of time. Examples are broken cobwebs, movement of earth, leaves covering growing vegetation, and disturbances to the insect world.

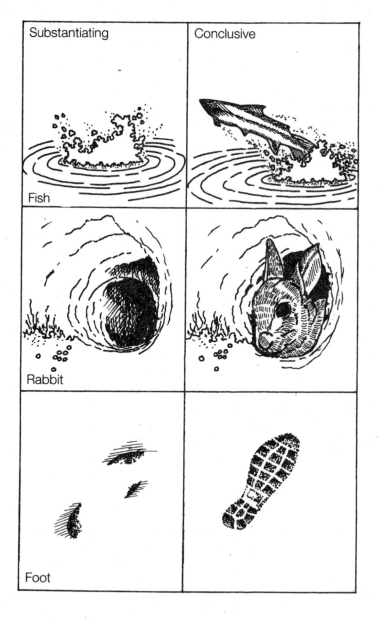

Figure 7 Substantiating and conclusive sign

Permanent sign   Sign is classed by a tracker as permanent when it is of a lasting nature – there is no specific time scale but rather a common sense approach is used to determine the correct classification. Permanent sign is very resistant to weathering, although even the hardest granite will eventually be eroded by rainwater, and man-made objects such as tin cans, newspapers and clothing will eventually weather or rot away. Also man may repair a broken fence or gate but this should be detected by the observant tracker. Examples are badger setts, fox earths, rabbit burrows, bird and animal nests, broken or cut vegetation, dead animals, broken fences and gates, discarded man-made objects.

HOW TO STUDY SIGN

Now we have an understanding of the various categories and classifications of sign, let's move on to a practical illustration of how a tracker reads sign.

For this example let us look at the process of studying the sign left after a human has passed through a leaf-covered area. The first sign that is located is usually the ground sign. The tracker has to decide whether it is human or animal. Once this is established, the approximate height and size of the quarry can be determined by the extent of the top sign – remember this is any sign above ankle height.

Initially the first sign must be studied carefully, that is, 'the first footprint'. This must be measured and recorded as a sketch. See figure 8 for the details which should be noted.

The approximate weight of the person may be found by comparing the depth of the sign left with that of your own imprint or the footprint of a known person with the same size foot. The experienced tracker will not jump to any conclusions at this stage about the weight of the person until he has seen other sign which gives an indication as to whether the quarry was carrying a load or not.

The length of pace may indicate whether the person is tall, short, or carrying a pack. Top sign will normally verify this sort of information.

Study the top layer of leaves, sorting out those that are bent or broken because they have been trodden on, remembering that some will be displaced. Mentally replace all or as many as possible of those displaced leaves and twigs. Pick up and

Figure 8   Details of the first print that should be recorded

examine each leaf in turn for what is called a straight edge. Remember where each leaf was taken from – see figure 9.

After removing and checking the top layer continue down to the next layer. If the conditions are wet this will be fairly pliable. Notice any distinctive bends that may indicate an edge of a boot.

Remove the next layer and study the earth itself. Look for squashed worm casts, indentations from twigs and nuts.

Figure 9   Studying sign in a leaf-strewn area

Establish the heel and toe and whether it is the left or right foot and, in the case of animals, whether it is the fore or rear.

Whatever the nature of the ground may be, always look up from the ground sign at frequent intervals. Where there are bushes and undergrowth bits of hair and fur, or shreds of clothing may be spotted. These will give a clue to the direction of the track and to the quarry's height and bulk.

SUMMARY

A good understanding of sign, and how to identify it is the vital skill which allows the tracker to build up the tracking picture. During the initial learning stages it is the most important part of visual tracking. With experience and practice locating and identifying sign will become much easier and what was once a closed book will open up and the track will come to life.

CHAPTER FOUR

Factors Affecting Sign

So much depends upon the state of the ground and the weather that it is very difficult to recognise the track under all circumstances. The difference between a track left by an animal or a man walking across a rocky outcrop and that which he leaves as he passes through an area with a clay-based soil is huge and yet it is the track of the same quarry.

The best way to meet this difficulty, and to teach yourself how to recognise a track under varying conditions and on different kinds of soil, is to practise continually. Make a habit of imagining, as you walk along, what sort of tracks would be left by a man or an animal on the environment through which you are passing.

As we progress on to the technical aspects of tracking you may find it useful to refer to the definitions in Chapter Two.

Sign is the crux of tracking. Sign, and consequently a visual tracker's ability to follow it, is influenced by four main factors:

- Spoor and sign left by other animals and vehicles
- Features of the terrain
- Climatic conditions
- Time

In general, all four factors are very closely tied and this fact has both advantages and disadvantages for the tracker. So it is important that you have an understanding of each of the four factors and how they interrelate.

THIRD PARTY SPOOR AND SIGN

Spoor and sign belong to one of three groups:

- You the tracker and your team
- The quarry which can be one or more animals, persons or vehicles
- A third party

During a pursuit the quarry's sign is the most important thing to consider. However, a tracker must consider other spoor and sign in the area and how it is going to affect the track of the quarry.

You the tracker can and should govern the movement of your own group so as not to foul the track of the quarry, but you have no control over the activities of any third party who has previously left sign in the area and may already have fouled the track.

A tracker must consider the animal life in the area and know how to identify the difference between animal and human sign. It is fairly easy to identify the differences between animal and human spoor. For example the majority of animals with hooves leave a distinctive 'chop' type mark as they move along a trail. This is caused by the shape of the hoof and the weight distribution. The hoof acts like a knife edge and the weight of the animal causes the hoof to cut into the ground. By contrast, humans tend to heel and toe their movements when walking, which is reflected in their spoor by an incised heel mark and a dragged part at the forward edge of the print where the toe scuffs the ground. Such identification is possible, even if the track advances across ground with a hard surface which does not allow a clear print – see Chapter Twenty-Two for a fuller exposition of animal prints.

There can be advantages and disadvantages to third party sign. For example, prints superimposed on a quarry's prints may assist the tracker in gauging the age of the track if he knows when the third party passed by. But, large groups of animals, such as flocks of sheep, or herds of cows may obliterate the sign of the quarry to such an extent that the tracker finds it impossible to continue any pursuit.

THE TERRAIN

The geographical features of the terrain may or may not assist the tracker. The following is a list of some of the major types of terrain which offer very distinctive attributes for the tracker:
- Grass and cultivated areas
- Rocky ground
- Sandy desert
- Primary forests
- Secondary forests and dense undergrowth
- Inland waterways and marshy areas

- The sea shore
- Snow-covered regions
- Urban and built-up areas

Each type of terrain presents the tracker with a new challenge.

Grass and cultivated areas

Although it is difficult to obtain any clear impression of individual pieces of sign on grass, a track through grass will show up very clearly. The bruised and trampled grass can be seen some distance ahead and it is quite easy to decide in which direction the track leads. If, on looking at a field, you see a track which looks lighter than the surrounding grass, then you can be certain that whatever has made the track has been going away from you. If, on the other hand, the track appears darker than the surrounding grass, then you can be certain that whatever has made the track has been coming towards the place where you are standing. This visual aid is a result of the way in which light is reflected back from the surface of the disturbed vegetation. The same feature can be seen when a lawn is mowed in alternate directions – there are strips of light and dark.

It is even easier to follow a track through grass that is wet with dew or light rain, or which is frosted.

Frequently, places will be found where the grass has been nibbled if your quarry is a grass-eating animal, or where the ribs in the sole of a man's boot has torn off a blade or two.

If the grass is high, that is, above ankle height, tracks are relatively easy to follow because the grass is knocked down and will stay down for some time, depending on the weather. The shorter the grass the more quickly it springs back into its original position.

The following points will assist when tracking in this type of country:

- Grass is normally trodden down and pointing in the direction in which the quarry is travelling – an example of pointers
- It presents a contrast in colour to the normal undergrowth when pressed down – an example of colour change
- If the grass has been wet with dew from the night before, the dew will be rubbed off by the passage of the quarry – an example of disturbance

- Mud or soil from footwear may appear on some of the grass – an example of transfer
- In dry grass broken and crushed blades and stems will be found and possibly footprints
- If new vegetation is showing through it indicates that it is an old track
- In very short grass, that is, up to ankle height, hoof, pad, claw and boots will damage the grass near the ground and invariably an impression will be found

Rocky ground

At first it would seem an almost impossible task to track someone across rocky ground but there are a considerable number of aids. The professional tracker does not expect to find a perfectly formed boot print at every pace.

The following features will help you to track over rocky ground:

- Impressions in any dust
- Displaced stones or twigs
- Different coloured spots from which stones have been moved
- Scratches and marks on the rock surface made by the quarry, for example, humans wearing boots will leave rubber scuff marks, and animals will leave nail scratch marks
- Brittle rock is easily chipped and some rocks crumble when walked on leaving a light patch
- Displaced rock chippings broken off by the quarry can be seen nearby
- The rocks may lend themselves to easy and obvious stepping-places
- Lichen rubbed off or marked
- Moss growing on rocks can be dislodged by foot, hand, claw, pad or hoof
- Vegetation growing in crevices may have been disturbed or bruised
- Differences in the colour of soil from where a stone has been displaced – if the ground is very dry there will be a lighter shade and if the ground is damp, a darker patch will show

- Stones may be displaced and the side which lay on the ground will show darker if the ground is damp and lighter if the ground is very dry
- Soil under stones or rocks which have been trodden on will bear witness to the pressure of the foot upon the ground and will be a different shade
- On sandstone, shoe and hoof marks tend to show dark colours
- Stones on the side of hills tend to move slightly or roll away when walked on – this action takes place irrespective of whether the quarry is walking up or down the slope
- Stones on a loose or soft surface are normally pressed in when walked upon, leaving either a ridge around the edge of the stone where it has forced the dirt out or a hole where the stone has been pushed below the surface of the ground
- Particles of stone sometimes catch in the sole of footwear and hoofs and are deposited further on – these can show up vividly against a contrasting background, this is a good example of transfer
- Squashed insects may be seen which have not yet been removed by other predator insects, such as ants or beetles – this will give a tracker experienced in the particular environment a very good indication of the time lapse between the passage of the quarry and the sighting of the sign. If insects which have been injured and immobilised by the quarry's tread are still alive it shows that the quarry passed through recently
- The quarry may be channelled by large rock formations which indicate to the tracker an obvious route
- Sign may be found in the area of soft ground near the base of large rocks and boulders

I hope that with the guidelines above the potential tracker will now see that what could at first sight appear to be a mission impossible is entirely feasible.

Sandy desert

Soft, deep sand or dust does not give a clear impression, for the sand or dust falls in around the sign blurring the edges and making it difficult to read with any accuracy.

The most significant aspect of tracking in sandy regions, especially in the desert dunes of areas such as the Sahara and the Empty Quarter, is the part played by the wind. Even the smallest, faintest track left in these areas can remain in existence for days and weeks, but the imprint of the tyres of a ten-ton truck can be completely obliterated in minutes by the strong desert winds that blow in certain seasons.

Anyone tasked to track in this sort of region must have a good understanding of the prevailing climatic conditions, and the effect of the diurnal heat changes on the hardness of the sand surface. A track laid during the early morning, when the surface can be concrete hard, may barely be visible whereas a few hours later the same quarry will leave deep indentations in the surface of the sand.

I have found, through experience, desert tracking to be the hardest even though to the casual observer it might appear an easy tracking environment.

Primary forest
Tracking through primary forests is without doubt the most satisfying of tracking environments. Here trackers will find many ways by which they can track since it includes both undergrowth and mature trees, live and dead vegetation, streams with muddy and sandy banks, moss carpeting the forest floor and rocks, and an abundance of animal life.

The potential of tracking through this medium did not escape the attention of the military planners during the post-colonial counter-insurgency wars in the jungle areas of South-East Asia – see the military tracking anecdotes in Chapter Eighteen.

During my attachment to the jungle warfare training establishment in Brunei, I made use of many of the following features of primary forests to assist me in my tracking exercises:

- Leaves on the forest floor when wet and disturbed will show much darker than those undisturbed
- Dry leaves when disturbed show a distinct dark brown on the underside in comparison with the biscuity colour of the bleached upper surface
- Some types of vegetation, either leaves or twigs, become very brittle when dead. These crack and break under the pressure of a quarry walking over them

- The underside of the green leaves of bushes, especially in the thick undergrowth on the edges of the forest, show up lighter in shade than the top of the leaf when it has been pushed aside or twisted by the passage of the quarry – this is a good example of both colour change and pointers
- Broken twigs give the experienced tracker a good indication of the time since they were damaged. Freshly broken twigs are generally a creamier colour at the break, this colour gets darker with time. A tracker may break the twig again to get an indication, by comparison, of how long it was since the original break occurred. Only by experiment and experience will the tracker be able to determine the age of the break
- Freshly broken green twigs usually retain the smell of sap for three to four hours
- Fallen and especially rotting trees will retain the impressions of any footprints
- Logs which have fallen across a path are usually scuffed by the quarry as he negotiates them and if he is careful to avoid this he will inevitably leave sign on either side of the log as he steps over it
- Roots crossing a path will show signs of having been walked on where they are bruised and bleeding
- Broken cobwebs across the path indicates the passage of animals or humans along the path and if a tracker were moving along a jungle trail first thing in the morning and the cobwebs were broken at head height it would be a very real indication of how close the tracking team were to the enemy
- Pine needles can be found in most European primary forests and a quarry passing over them will leave an expansive but shallow depression – similar to when a child stands on a soft duvet cover on a bed

When working in these surroundings the tracker student must be trained and encouraged to look through the forest and the vegetation and not at it. The jungle can easily become a mesmerising green blanket which retains its secrets. The jungle tracker through careful observation, analysis, and deduction is able to transform the enshrouding blanket into a light translucent veil which eventually fades away completely, leaving a clear, well-focused picture of the events.

Secondary forests and dense undergrowth

The sixty-metre high primary forest trees of the typical virgin jungle produce a canopy of vegetation which prevents the sunlight penetrating to the jungle floor. The result is that in primary forests one finds the jungle giants spaced at fairly large intervals with very little growth in between. This type of jungle is often referred to as being clean – it is a pleasurable environment in which to work.

Secondary forests result when the primary forest has been cleared, either by migrating slash and burn aboriginal cultivators over hundreds of years, or by industrial logging companies over a few months. The vegetation is very thick due to the constant sunlight it receives.

The significance to the tracker is that any large animal passing through this type of undergrowth cannot fail to leave a lot of sign. When tracking in it the main points to watch for are:

- Broken branches, leaves and roots
- Vegetation facing in the direction in which the quarry has gone – these are pointers
- Footprints on the ground – grass does not grow in this environment
- Tunnels made by the passage of the quarry
- Broken cobwebs
- Pieces of fur and other animal coatings caught on the tangle of vegetation or on the thorns and spikes produced by some of the plants

Although this is a very arduous type of area to operate in for the visual tracker there is an abundance of sign, as it is impossible, even for the most devious enemy, not to leave evidence of his passage.

Inland waterways and marshy areas

Under this type of terrain I include rivers, streams, ponds, lakes, canals, marshes, and bogs. Contrary to general belief, tracking is possible where these circumstances exist. The wetter areas are very difficult to track in, except for shallow or still water where footprints may show up, or when following a very fresh track, where splashes on rocks and vegetation and muddy water will be obvious telltale indications of the quarry's presence.

Signs to assist the tracker in these sorts of region are:

- Footprints on the bank where the quarry has entered and exited
- Skid, slip and slide marks on banks – these will show as very distinctive colour changes
- Footprints in shallow water – the tracker must examine the river bed looking for colour change, being very careful to avoid fouling the sign
- Stones on river beds are covered in a type of sediment. Therefore when the stone has been trodden on there is a definite colour change
- Mud churned up discolouring the water
- Rocks splashed with water in a quiet running stream – this is transfer
- Places on the bank where a person has sat down to take his shoes off, or to put them back on – this results in flattening of the area
- Foliage growing over a stream may be disturbed or broken
- Entry and exit points are usually obvious and channel the quarry, therefore time should be spent looking for these

As can be seen from this list tracking is possible around inland waterways but I would like to give a word of warning, especially to the adult with responsibilities for training young people. All waterways are potentially dangerous to the inexperienced and animals especially can lead the unwary into trouble. Remember it's quite easy for small animals, such as foxes, rabbits, badgers, and birds to walk on top of a bog without sinking and they can also easily swim across a canal, a pond, a river, or a lake.

The sea shore

The sea shore has many features in common with sandy deserts and also inland waterways – the unique salient feature for the tracker is the effect which the tides may have on his task. Although the encroaching sea obscures sign, with a knowledge of the tides, the tracker can on occasions place sign within a specific time bracket.

Soft, damp sand will leave a very clear-cut impression which will be easy to distinguish and follow. It will remain apparently fresh for a considerable time. But, dry sand is badly affected by strong winds, as I stated above in the section on sandy desert regions.

The main points to be considered are as follows:

- If the surface is inclined to be wet and hard, the footprint is very clear
- If the surface is soft, the footprints will be quite deep
- In the early morning and late afternoon the walls of the impression may cast a deep shadow because of the lack of relief and obstructions often characteristic of coastal areas

Snow-covered regions

After a fresh fall of snow anything that moves across it will leave a patently obvious track. This is probably the tracker's easiest tracking task.

The following are some of the distinctive features of tracking through snow:

- Secondary snow falls – even if there is another fall of snow on top of the quarry's sign, under the right conditions you can still follow the track by the shadow under the surface layer
- Hardness of the surface – this governs the prominence of the sign
- Differences in sign made by the same animal – this phenomenon occurs when, for instance, an animal leaves a recognisable, normal, clear track in snow an inch or two deep which has a hard surface, but in deep soft snow the whole appearance of the track will alter. On hard snow a rabbit's track is easy to identify, but in soft snow it is very difficult to reconcile the large foot prints he makes with his size. Again, animals which do not leave a tail-mark on hard ground may leave a very distinctive and initially confusing tail-mark in soft deep snow

I have not included ice-covered regions in this section because the skill required for tracking under such conditions are more akin to those recorded above in the section on Rocky Ground.

Urban and built-up areas

The skills required for tracking in built-up areas are not the sole preserve of the large town or inner-city because the tracker following a quarry through a predominantly rural area may suddenly find himself in a large farm complex, a disused airfield, or some such man-made feature.

The significant feature of areas such as these are the hard artificial surfaces of which roads and railway lines are made and over which the quarry will move.

Fortunately, there is a great deal of commonality between built-up areas and other areas in which the tracker has to practise his skills – for instance there are many grassed areas and unsurfaced footpaths.

Invariably, though, tracking in built-up areas will involve foul tracks and will slow down most trackers. However, the tracker although slowed to pace tracking may speed up his pursuit by carrying out a process of track isolation through the following:

- Look for exit and entry points
- Searching likely areas – see Chapter Sixteen
- Presence of particular sign pattern

And a tracker following a track into a built-up area should be aware of the following points about the quarry:

- He may have a rendez-vous with someone
- He may be friendly with the local population
- He may live in the area

THE CLIMATE

The student of tracking has to familiarise himself with the effects of the weather and climatic conditions on spoor and sign.

The three climatic factors which affect the track are:

- Direct sunlight
- Strong wind
- Heavy precipitation

These are all factors which will adversely affect the sign of a track. The degree to which this will happen varies and depends upon:

- The strength of the element
- Whether they were working in combination or separately
- The duration the element impinged on the sign
- The type of terrain

Generally speaking, tracks sheltered from direct sunlight, strong wind and heavy rain can still be recognised days, if not weeks, after they were made.

Direct sunlight

This causes sign to return to normal more quickly. Although we have already seen how in certain circumstances the presence of sunlight can help the tracker to determine the quarry's direction of movement – a light path indicating movement away, a dark path indicating movement towards.

Strong winds

The wind encourages disturbed vegetation to return to its original position. This is particularly true of long grasses and tall cereal crops like corn, wheat, and barley. When a strong wind blows, any grass shoots displaced by the quarry tend to be tugged back up into their original position. In these circumstances a tracker will primarily be following ground sign and if you look at the lower part of the grass stem you will find that it will be broken and pointing in the direction in which the quarry travelled.

Strong winds may also conceal ground sign as debris is blown about.

For the observant, aware tracker the effects of the wind can be an advantage. It may have blown dust, dried grass, straws, leaves or other debris over the marks. This feature, coupled with the observation as to when the weather was windy, will give you a clue as to the time the sign was made.

It is this type of detail which is always important. And it is this type of awareness of his surroundings that sets the good tracker apart, for he is continually monitoring significant changes and remembering what has happened.

Being aware of your surroundings and the interplay of factors is the reason why any tracker working a woodland area, whether it be jungle or temperate, is always alert to the dangers of deadfalls. Deadfalls are the result of old, dead or rotten wood suddenly being displaced by the wind or rain. As they come crashing through the smaller, flimsier branches nearer the ground the unwary have little time to react.

Heavy precipitation

This will wash out some sign very quickly, particularly ground sign, and is probably the tracker's greatest enemy.

On the other hand, if there has been only a light shower, spots of rain may have pitted the sign, thus giving the tracker an additional clue as to the time it was made (see Chapters Fourteen and Fifteen for a full explanation of judging the age of sign and deductive skills.)

TIME

Time is the fourth of the factors which affect sign. To be able to assess the time bracket between when a spoor mark was made and when it is found is one of the crucial tracking skills. Only experience and practice will enable the tracker to judge accurately when sign was made.

Out of all the four factors affecting sign, time is probably the one which proves the greatest challenge to the tracker. The following practical anecdote illustrates what I mean. The owner of a sheep station in Australia was riding with one of his stockmen. They were looking for a flock which was known to have passed through the area over a week ago. The owner saw many tracks, assumed they were made by his flock, and suggested they should follow them. The aboriginal stockman contradicted him reasoning, 'no, these tracks were only made two days ago.'

It would have been easy to be misled by the obvious tracks if the stockman hadn't taken into account all the facts and then applied them to his observations.

The following are some of the main indicators of timing:

- The track in question may cross other tracks of which the timing is known if, for instance, they are made by humans whom you have identified and of whom you know the movements, or in a similar way they may be animal tracks whose habits are familiar to you
- Insects and worms that have worked across the marks can be useful to the locally experienced tracker
- The heat retained by the remains of fires, food and faeces
- Grass and other vegetation that has been bent will spring into normal place again in a few hours

- Broken vegetation will wither and die at set rates depending on the type of plant and the climatic conditions
- Observation and the ability to recall changes in the weather will also enable you to assess timings – for example a boot print with only a very small amount of water in it when it has been raining heavily for several hours would indicate the quarry is very close
- Water running back into a boot print on the edge of a puddle also helps to establish the passage of time
- The drying rate of soil which has been disturbed and exposed to sunlight
- The obliteration rate of sign by strong winds
- A knowledge of the characteristics of various soils also helps the tracker to assess the time lapse. Most clay-based soils or earth will keep the impression longer and more distinctly than loamy or sandy soils

To sum up, the tracker must be aware that the four factors which affect sign do not influence the track independently of each other. They work in unison on the sign and spoor to weather it and to alter its nature. Sometimes one of the factors becomes dominant and at other times it is the interplay of the factors which produces the changes in the original sign.

CHAPTER FIVE

The Attributes of a Tracker

A story I read as a boy has, I suppose, become a part of my personal philosophy. A party of academics and explorers were carrying out a scientific expedition in the interior of Australia in an area which in those days was appropriately known as the Great Thirstland. The only reason they came out of the area alive was because a little aboriginal girl was accompanying them.

The work of the expedition had been abandoned. The members of the group were dying of thirst and were desperately searching for water. The girl had noticed some ants creeping up the stem of a tree and making their way into a small hole in the bark. She realised that there would be a purpose behind their activity. She pushed a twig into the hole to explore. She discovered that water was contained in the tree trunk. She then stripped the bark from some green twigs so that they formed a succession of small tubes. She fitted them together to form a drinking straw and passed the end of this tube down through the hole into the tree enabling each one of the party to suck up their fill of water.

An uneducated fourteen-year-old, aboriginal girl saved the lives of the scientists. She had been able to perform her mercy mission due to powers of observation, deduction and ingenuity. It hadn't been the sophisticated knowledge which the members of the expedition had possessed that had saved them, but the natural knowledge of one who had been brought up to observe the essentials of life.

Trackers need to develop the sort of expertise that came so naturally to this young aboriginal girl. Good trackers are characterised by their outstanding ability to observe, remember, select, analyse and comprehend. The tracker when observing needs to look beyond mere recognition and go on to observe every detail. He must then remember all he's seen, smelt, heard, felt and possibly tasted, and usually without resorting to making notes.

The salient points are then selected or collated for analysis. All this has to be done almost instinctively before he can arrive at correct deductions and an accurate comprehension of what has occurred.

THE QUALITIES OF A GOOD TRACKER

Anyone using tracking skills will soon realise that he is called on to make many decisions. He will be required to draw heavily on his training and experience. But above all else he will need acute observation, patience, and persistence.

He has to understand nature. He has to keep himself at a high standard of physical fitness. He has to have a good memory with which to retain and piece together the many small parcels of information – the sign left along a track.

The job of potential trackers is to think for themselves, to reason out statements for themselves, to discover the whys and wherefores of an activity for themselves. They may be helped to a certain extent by the advice and experience of others, especially if they are a member of a tracking team, but they should not become dependent on others. Trackers need to be self-sufficient, free-spirits. They do not blindly accept the obvious explanations.

To be a competent tracker you must develop the following qualities:

- Patience
- An inquisitive mind
- Honesty
- Perseverance
- Acute observation
- All five senses must be well attuned
- Above average endurance
- Above average standard of field craft
- Mental and physical determination
- A good knowledge of the local fauna and flora
- Curiosity

Contrary to common belief, people are not born with the natural instincts of a tracker. A tracker is not a special breed of person. Trackers come from all backgrounds and nationalities. Being country-reared, although an initial advantage, does not necessarily exclude the city dweller from becoming a competent tracker. Through dedication and hard work it is possible for anyone to become proficient in the art of tracking.

Generally speaking, a tracker is normally most efficient in his country of origin. Of course in a new country his effectiveness will depend entirely on his ability to adjust to a new environment. Once this is achieved a tracker is able to perform to his or her maximum efficiency. The sooner he gains first-hand knowledge of his area of operation, the better equipped he will be to follow through each tracking task successfully.

SELF-KNOWLEDGE

Good trackers are aware of their limitations, both in terms of fatigue and tracking ability. In short, they are honest with themselves and others.

Firstly, they do not track on when tired because they know a tired tracker easily loses the track, becomes noisy and clumsy in his movements, and is less likely to see the quarry.

Secondly, they know their skill level and are confident without being over confident. When a track becomes difficult and you are straining to follow the track, it is easy to see sign where none exists. Students of visual tracking are particularly prone to this tendency in their early days. Be aware and do not bluff yourself and others into thinking you are following the quarry when you are following an imaginary track.

I was told on my tracking course that I had to be prepared to follow a track for days and that it could be hard frustrating work with many false trails, but that if I was destined to be a good tracker, eventually everything would click into place. There were others on the course who, by their own admission, couldn't track their way out of a paper bag but their time wasn't wasted because these soldiers over the eight-week course began to realise that, in a war situation, a trained tracker can be deadly. They automatically started eliminating the sign that they left behind, realising this could hinder a tracker.

PSYCHOLOGY OF THE QUARRY

Attempt to picture in your mind the party making the track. Try and get into their skin and into their mind. Your quarry may be leading the existence of a hunted animal. Don't underestimate his skill. He will be forcing himself to move very quietly and cautiously. He will be using all his skill and cunning to deceive you. Remember the possibility of a purposely misleading trail. Remember he may be in fear of his life and therefore a great threat to you.

As you build up the information about the quarry it is as though a transparent, ghostly image starts to take on a shape and then eventually you clothe and equip the person and finally enter into his mind. When a tracker is extremely adept at his skill he can anticipate the quarry's next move. This is not only of importance to the military or police tracker, but can be a life-saver for the mountain rescue team. As the tracker deduces the state of mind of the person being searched for by analysing the sign he is leaving it is a small step from here for a tracker to foresee what decisions the victim will make at various junctures.

This knowledge of the quarry helps the military or police tracker develop his sixth sense and become aware of danger as he approaches the quarry. Needless to say, this cannot be achieved in a base camp surrounded by his fellow men and all the trappings of civilisation – it is a result of being in the field and tuning into the environment over prolonged periods.

THE FIVE SENSES

Good trackers have to learn one vital lesson early on in their development, no matter how the skills are applied: by hunter, conservationist, police, search and rescue, gamekeeper or military tracker. Trackers must let nothing escape their attention.

It takes a good deal of practice before a potential tracker can get into the habit of noting everything before him. Development of the memory and mental processes are key. Without constant training and practice the information provided by the sign becomes difficult if not impossible to decipher.

There seems to be no doubt that civilisation has a tendency to dull all our five senses – sight, hearing, smell, taste and touch. They become dull because we are not so dependent upon them, and because the opportunities for their use have been lessened. Town-dwellers especially suffer in this respect. Vision is limited by walls and roofs, and sight is harmed by artificial light. Hearing is dulled by the continual grind and roar of modern traffic. Smell is clouded by the fumes of petrol and oil that hang about the streets and by all the other pollutants associated with a modern city. Taste, which is so closely allied to smell, is very rarely fully engaged, except by a few skilled trades and professions. For the tracker all five senses are important. Sign is not confined to things that can be seen, but includes also things that can be heard, smelt, tasted and touched.

Again, not only have the senses to record an impression, automatically or sub-consciously, but the tracker must train himself to remember it. An observation is useless unless it is crystallised into the memory. Observation cannot be divorced from memory if the tracker is going to benefit from the raw material his senses have given him.

PART TWO

The Pursuit

CHAPTER SIX

Observation Indoors

Observation is so closely linked to tracking as to be inseparable. Therefore, I think it only right that before I proceed to tracking drills proper I should spend some time explaining how to develop the powers of observation. This training can be undertaken in two stages. This chapter will deal with the first stage – the indoor stage. It is an added bonus for the teacher or youth group leader that you can progress with your tracker training course during the evenings or when the weather precludes outdoor activities.

A great deal of the indoor training revolves around the memory and observation training technique known as Kim's Game. This can mistakenly be considered merely as a party game but I can assure you that it is used as the basis of memory and observation skills training by some of the best surveillance units in the military.

Kim was the hero of the eponymous tale by Kipling. He was being trained for his secret service work on behalf of the British Raj – the Great Game. His training was conducted using stones on a tray. Now slides and video clips are used but essentially the training is the same. The advantages of Kim's Game are that it is easy to conduct, it can be carried out indoors, and it is directly relevant to tracking in that it develops and sharpens both observational skills and, just as importantly, the memory.

Before I lay out the practical details for conducting Kim's Game as a training session, I think it would be beneficial if I explain some of the basic principles of memory.

MEMORY TRAINING

If you are aware of some of the key processes that take place when you use your memory you can take steps to improve its efficiency. It is worth spending some time studying the best ways to enhance your own memory. Although individuals are different, there are certain broad principles which should be borne in mind.

Memory is the process of storing and retrieving information, or retention and recall.

Storage techniques:
- Association – the more facts that are associated with the object the better the chance of the object being remembered
- Groupings or clusters – organise in your mind similar items in a group
- Visualisation – imagine some visually vivid image of the items you are trying to remember

Retrieval techniques:
- The Greek system of a familiar room – imagine a tour around a room you know intimately and associate the facts you are trying to remember with items in the room
- Knot in the tie or some item which is out of place – this immediately triggers the memory
- Mnemonics – produce your own mnemonic lists

Recall is state-dependent, that is, we recall better if the state we learnt the facts in is the same as the one in which we are trying to recall them.

Memory is either short- or long-term. Phone numbers are designed to use the short-term memory function they are usually about six digits long.

The physiological processes that come into play to transfer from short-term to long-term are beyond the scope of this book but it is worth noting from a practical point of view that there are two sorts of memory. For instance, you may think that you have remembered some feature of the sign you observed three hours before but it may have only impinged on the short-term memory and you may not be able to recall it later.

Another important part of the memory which we must be aware of is its opposite – forgetting.

This is defined as when information becomes inaccessible. It may be inaccessible because it is no longer in store or it cannot be retrieved. Forgetting is a vital function, otherwise we would be overloaded with every sensory stimulus that impinged on us.

Factors involved with forgetting:

- Time
- Interference – similar things interfere with each other, e.g. two vehicle registration numbers
- Distortions – due to what the person regards as most important. We try to reconstruct events into a previously recognisable pattern, as opposed to what actually happened, e.g. if a man passes a parcel to a librarian, we record it as being a book because that is what we are expecting
- Memories can be entirely false
- Memories are not fixed but change over time and can also be affected by other memory inputs

We all have a memory and it is a faculty which, with practice, can be improved. Exercises which allow us to make better use of our memories, conciously or subconciously, are:

- Fantasy – a green limousine is remembered as a crocodile and the three passengers as three birds on its back
- Visualisation – it is easier to recall concrete images, so try and see the vivid red of the pillar box which the man went to before he strode across the wide street to the sparkling lights of the restaurant
- Association – to remember a series of key words in the correct sequence link them in your mind to articles in a room with which you are very familiar, ensuring that they are in the sequence you would see walking through the room
- Exaggeration – this is ideal for remembering the features of a person, if the person has long fingers they are remembered in an elongated fashion similar to how a cartoonist or caricaturist depicts his subjects

It is interesting that these are all positive acts; memorising information is not passive. We are not sponges and although individuals have natural preferences for memorising – some are more aurally aware than others, while some find the sense of smell an evocative trigger – all of these exercises can be actively employed to improve memory storage and recall. For a detailed description of these techniques I recommend you study *A Question of Memory* by D. Berglas and G. L. Playfair.

There are good reasons for a potential tracker to study and improve his memory. As you move along the track there will be many details of the sign. Some of these may appear irrelevant as you follow the three to five items of key sign, but when linked up to something further along the pursuit they may become a vital piece of the jigsaw which indicate something very important about your quarry.

For instance you may be following the key sign of a booted man down a much used track where there is a great deal of other sign. But every mile or so a slight oval indentation about three or four inches in length appears alongside his boot print. If this was overlooked or not remembered you may not realise the man was armed – that indentation being the butt of his rifle which he rested on the ground as he paused to read his map.

Exercise your memory. Engage your powers of retention and recall positively during your daily life. It isn't a faculty which gets worn out!

KIM'S GAME

The basic standard layout for Kim's Game is twenty small objects placed at random on a cloth. The items should be from a variety of uses and backgrounds. The students are allowed to study them for one minute and then the articles are covered. They are then asked to write down accurate and full descriptions of as many of the items that they can remember.

From the start an emphasis should be placed upon accurate and full descriptions to engender an attention to detail. For instance 'a small metal object' is not sufficient for the description of a key. The type of description that should be aimed at is, 'a Yale-type key, bronze coloured, with a slight crack ½ way down its length'.

As a build up fewer, larger objects can be used. The exposure time can be lengthened and the students can be asked to give verbal descriptions. Advice which the instructor can give to the student after the first few attempts might be:

- Count the number of items
- Study the smaller things first
- Group the objects

- Don't hurry – keep calm

The instructor can vary the standard format of the game along many lines:

- Vary the types of items
- Alter the method of arrangement – use the floor, suspend them from the ceiling, scatter them around the room
- Use slides and video clips
- The game can be played as a team
- The game can be sprung on a group of people without any kind of warning, or in the midst of another activity
- Interfere with the memory by introducing another task, or by planning a time lapse before writing the results down

Other variations on the theme are:

- A fleeting observation of one single article, for example, a look at an envelope reveals the postmark (foreign or domestic), the writing, marks on the envelope, the size, the shape (flat or bulging), the flap, the stamp, the colour, and the quality of the paper
- Asking participants to remember the details of a room
- Before and after situations – 'What is wrong?' or 'What is missing?'
- The use of distance by holding up articles at the opposite end of the room
- Colour can be utilised in two ways – firstly, to make an article insignificant by the fact that it is surrounded by other articles of more brilliant colouring, and secondly to aid the memory by grouping things of the same colour

These changes of conditions are an important factor in the advanced application of Kim's Game. They prepare the student for the reality of an incident – you are not warned beforehand that something which requires observation is going to appear or to happen. If you have acquired the habit of observation you will have recorded it, if not, you will be left startled and remember nothing.

THE USE OF OTHER SENSES

Most people's senses are dominated by visual stimuli but, as has been stressed previously, the tracker must be open to gain information from all five senses. It may be one of the seemingly less significant senses, such as taste or touch, which provides the conclusive evidence, for example, are the ashes in the fire hot or cold?

HEARING

The use of sight is not the only means by which the quarry's presence and activities can be detected. A trained tracker can gather valuable information by using his sense of hearing to locate the quarry. Trackers need to be trained to actively listen for sounds. They have to be able to differentiate between the natural and the unnatural.

The following are some of the common sounds a tracker may hear:

- Metal against metal
- Vehicle movement
- Human movement
- Chopping
- Human noises
- Birds calling
- Foxes barking/howling
- Animals rutting/digging
- Birds flying
- Fish, birds and animals splashing

Visual information is presented directly to the observer. Although many of the above sounds will be instantly recognisable to a trained tracker, the use of hearing requires deduction on the part of the hearer. Only with practice and imaginative training will accurate information be gathered through the sense of hearing.

The sense of hearing can again be sharpened by games which can be conducted indoors. Noises Out is perhaps the best known and the most useful. All that is required in this game is for someone who is concealed behind a screen, or behind a door, to make a series of noises, either by dropping articles on the floor, or by moving articles about, or by using their mouth to make the sounds. The students are then asked to give their interpretation of what the sound represented, e.g. men whispering, a vehicle starting up, a man digging, cattle moving. The instructor can use tape recordings but it is probably still better concealing the source of the noise by a screen and interspersing non-recorded noises in the sequence.

Hunt the Watch is another game which can be used to stimulate the concentration on hearing. Everyone is blindfolded and they have to search for a ticking watch. This game teaches some of the rudiments of stalking, and brings home the importance of keeping quiet and of moving quietly.

This game helps develop a sense of direction by ear which can be practised by various other means. For example, the group can sit in a wide circle with one of their number, blindfolded, in the centre. He has to identify both the nature and direction of any sound made by the other members of the group.

Again, the elements of surprise should be brought into the training. During a lesson, plan for a sudden noise to be made outside the room. And then ask, 'Now note down all you can about that noise.'

Important elements in describing noises are the tone and the rhythm. A potential tracker should be able to say whether one note was lower or higher than another.

SMELL

It is a known fact that hot air rises during the day and cold air sweeps down the valleys and spurs at night. Therefore, smells drift uphill in the daytime and downhill at night. It is helpful for you to know the type of smells that occur and that are made by you or your quarry. Taking this point further, the sense of smell can be a double-edged weapon in a tracking scenario. This point will be reiterated in the chapters on stalking and on military tracking.

One method of training the sense of smell is to surreptitiously introduce a noticeable and characteristic smell into the room during another activity – you record the reactions and comments. This will at least make the students aware of the necessity of keeping all their senses alert.

Items which can be introduced are:

- Burnt paper
- An oily rag
- Fish and chip papers
- Cigarette smoke

TASTE

Taste is related to and dependent on the sense of smell but the only relevance that it has to tracking is that if your taste buds are impaired by spicy foods it may also affect your sense of smell. It is all linked to having all your senses keyed up to a high pitch so that you are fully alert to your environment.

TOUCH

Touch is an interesting and overlooked sense with which a tracker can gain valuable information, especially with regards to texture and heat.

Cooking areas and sleeping areas can render a great deal of information about the age of the sign and how long the sites were occupied by the texture of soil – is it fresh or old? And if the occupation was more recent – how warm the ground is around the cooking and sleeping areas.

There is an interesting, although unsavoury, story about a French Foreign Legion tracker in their war against the Algerian rebels. When he came across human faeces he would test its age by poking his finger into it. Whether heat was retained inside and/or near the surface gave him some indication as to when the man defecated and therefore an indication of whether the enemy was close.

Detection exercises based on the use of touch not only lead to familiarity with shape and feel but also encourage trackers to use their deductive powers to gather information. For youngsters blindfold obstacle races indoors are amusing and useful. Another exercise in touch is to let two blindfolded potential trackers loose in a room to find each other, and let the others watch in complete silence. Those looking on will also learn a lot about feeling their way in the dark – one of the most important aspects being that when one sense is restricted, others compensate and therefore in this exercise hearing and smell will come into play.

Another indoor exercise for the potential tracker is to find his way about in the dark, first of all in a known room and then in a strange room, or one in which the furniture has been rearranged. The fire service practise such drills with the very serious aim of being able to locate and rescue people in smoke-filled premises.

The identification of various objects by touch alone should be frequently practised. The articles need not necessarily be small. It is possible to identify a person by passing the fingers lightly over the face. The blind can do this very readily, just as they learn to identify a person by the sound of his voice, or even the sound of his footsteps.

In time, after much practice, it will be found that it is possible to sense obstacles in the way before they are even touched.

I have attempted to demonstrate, especially to the adult responsible for training young people, that there is a great deal of scope for exercises related to tracking that can be carried out either in the winter evenings or during bad weather.

The subject of describing faces and individuals will be dealt with in a Chapter Eight but, as will be seen, it also affords great scope and opportunities for indoor work.

A tracker must remember, that his senses are his most valuable assets. It is important that all trackers continually exercise all their five senses – sight, hearing, smell, touch and taste. They should avoid activities and habits which detune their faculties.

When the senses are at a high pitch not only does the tracker recognise the sign of his quarry faster but his life is lived at a heightened state as he becomes more aware of his environment.

CHAPTER SEVEN

Observation Out-of-Doors

Both the youth group leader and the military tracking instructor will find that as the training moves out-of-doors the students will become more interested. For the student the training and exercises become more closely associated with tracking proper.

With visual training skills out-of-doors there is one very important difference that has to be brought home to the potential tracker – visual training, now, is training to observe coupled with the knowledge of how to conceal yourself.

Out-of-doors observation has an added difficulty in that the range of vision varies. In some types of terrain, for instance, the sand seas of the large deserts, it is practically limitless, whereas in scrub or secondary jungle it is very restricted.

Those who are accustomed to live in open spaces have usually much keener eyesight than those who live in towns. And the specific environment affects the ability to observe over the full range. For instance, the desert-dwelling Bedouin has a remarkably clear long vision, whereas jungle aborigines have a keen eye for the detail of sign.

The town-dwelling Westerner can adapt but he must be aware of what he is trying to do and his limitations. However he can make remarkable progress in a limited time. He will find that his learning curve is exponential. He will achieve a great deal at first, so long as he persists, but to emulate fully the Dyak or Iban trackers from South-East Asia would take him years of living in their environment.

There is an important lesson of observation to be learned from the following story. Common sense and a little reflection will often suggest to you the most likely places in which to look. Whilst in Dhofar with the SAS in the early 'seventies I became embroiled in a gentle challenge. One of the local hill tribesmen with whom we were operating tried, good naturedly, to get the upper hand of the foreign soldier by asking me how many goats were on the opposite mountainside. It was hardly possible to make out that there were any goats there at all, let alone count them. I could only make out a few whitish specks but not to be outdone, after admitting I couldn't count all the goats, I told him where the goat herders were, how many there were, and who they were.

I knew that the goat herders would be women and that there would be two of them – for company and as chaperones for each other. I couldn't actually see them but I guestimated that in the heat of the day they would be two black figures huddled under the largest, shadiest tree on the uphill side of the flock.

A look through the binoculars showed this to be correct.

Observe
Remember
Select and analyse
Comprehend and deduce

The use of sight is the primary means by which a tracker gathers and accumulates information, but seeing is more than just a question of looking. An understanding of why things are seen will assist a tracker in searching and detecting the quarry and its sign, and also help him to conceal himself. There are six factors which attract attention and determine why things are seen – see figure 10.

SHAPE

Personal equipment and the human body are familiar outlines to us all. They can be recognised instantly, particularly when they are in contrast to their surroundings. Distinctive shapes stand out and are more easily detected, for example someone wearing a raincoat, a hat, wellington boots, or carrying an umbrella or a shotgun. Remember your shape and the quarry's shape can be easily disguised by standing in front of the appropriate background.

SHADOW

Shadows are cast in sunlight, moonlight, and artificial light. An object casts a shadow which may give away its presence. On the other hand, an object that is concealed in other shadows is harder to detect and does not cast a shadow of its own. The

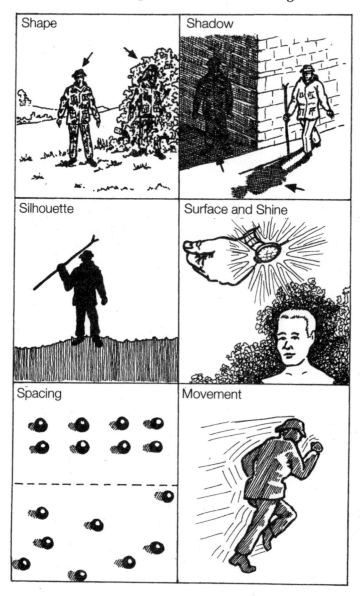

Figure 10 The six factors which attract attention

tracking student must be aware that as the sun, moon or artificial light moves, so do the shadows. Objects which were concealed by shadow may now be revealed, as they themselves cast their own distinctive shadow, or as they come out of the obscuring shadow.

There is another category of shadow and that is contained shadow. Contained shadow is that which is within a space, for example a hut, a room, a cave, or in a tent. It is normally darker than other shadows and can therefore attract attention. You will have seen this type of shadow depicted in detective films where all that is seen of the murderer with his upraised arm and knife is his shadow inside the room or the tent – see figure 11.

Figure 11   Contained shadow

At this point I think it is worth mentioning a significant point about shadows that relates specifically to sign. When a person walks over a carpet of leaves, they pile up in the direction of the movement. Depending on the light, a shadow will be visible, cast by this build-up of leaves.

SILHOUETTE
An object silhouetted against a contrasting background is conspicuous – smooth flat backgrounds such as water, snow, fields, or most extreme of all, the sky. An object may be silhouetted if it is against a contrasting background, for example, dark objects against a light background and vice versa.

SURFACE AND SHINE
If the colour and texture of the surface of an object contrasts with its surroundings it will be conspicuous. Shiny objects and white skin contrast violently with most backgrounds.

SPACING
Nature very rarely, if ever, spaces objects regularly. Therefore, the tracker should be alert to regularly spaced objects, even if they

appear natural. Apart from the obvious explanation of trees and bushes planted by man, the items may be more sinister camouflaged objects.

MOVEMENT

Sudden movement attracts the eye. This is easily demonstrated by half-concealing a number of people and inviting others to spot them. They will do so with difficulty while those concealed remain still, but when they move they will spot them easily. Sudden movement is easily seen, as will be realised when you come to practise stalking.

OBSERVATION TECHNIQUES

Now we understand why objects are seen we are able to study the next subject which is the proper use of our eyes. This may seem a simple affair but if you have a technique on which to concentrate you will not fall into the trap of looking and not seeing. In basic military training the instructor often spots the raw recruit whose head is turning to and fro as he patrols along on exercise. He seems to be alert but nothing that his gaze falls upon registers in his brain – he is looking without seeing. Consequently he will not be able to remember anything from which to deduce any conclusions – as a tracker he is worse than useless. There are two interrelated techniques – scanning and searching.

Scanning

This is a general and systematic examination of an area to detect any unusual or significant object or movement. To scan an area the following actions are recommended.

Divide the area into:
- Foreground
- Middle distance
- Far distance

Note: the size of the half-circle in figure 12 can be any size depending on the tracker's observational ability and the visibility.

Scan each area horizontally, starting with the foreground. To obtain maximum efficiency move the head in short overlapping movements. Moving the head as opposed to the eyes will

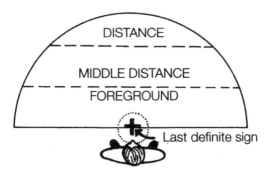

Figure 12   How the tracker divides the area for scanning

minimise eye fatigue. The speed at which scanning is carried out will depend on the type of ground being observed, that is, whether it is open or close country. When the horizontal scanning is complete, scan along the line of the features which are angled away from the observation position.

As a tracker your eyes scan from about five to ten metres out until sign is located. When you scan your head and eyes must keep on moving slowly from side to side and in a figure of eight pattern this is especially important in close country such as, secondary forest. This assists the tracker in looking through and not at the vegetation. Having picked up marks or signs, then move closer to inspect.

Searching
This is the next phase and may take place at any stage during the scanning. Any suspected movement or object which is spotted during the scanning requires an immediate more thorough visual study – a visual search of the area as opposed to a physical search.

If you are observing for movement it is better to stare at a place for a while and only move the head and eyes occasionally. Anything which moves will then attract the eye.

WHERE TO LOOK
Sign is easier to find in some places than others. The following are places where sign will be most obvious:
- Near the banks of rivers
- On muddy and sandy patches
- In high grass or thick undergrowth

- On steep hillsides
- On the edges of clearings
- Where obstacles have to be crossed

WHAT TO LOOK FOR

As you are scanning and searching you should remember each of the factors which make an object visible:

- Shape
- Shadow
- Silhouette
- Surface/Shine
- Spacing
- Movement

ON THE MOVE

Your eyes, ears and nose are constantly monitoring the environment. Every few minutes, depending on how close you suspect the quarry to be, and certainly not less often than every ten minutes, you must stop and listen.

Eyes must be trained to disregard the general pattern of foliage immediately to the front and to look through rather than at it. Another invaluable tactic is to get down on the ground and look through the undergrowth for any sign or sighting of the quarry.

You have to survey both near and far and inspect objects both large and small. When any unusual sign or sound is noted you must freeze quickly and silently. There should be no further movement until you have investigated.

BEFORE AND AFTER STUDIES

This is the application of very detailed observation to determine whether the quarry has entered an area or not. The basis of this technique is an in-depth study of what could be termed a micro-area to establish what its appearance is in its undisturbed state compared to the same area when the quarry has passed through it.

The format for this study is a description of the area in its pristine condition – the original state. This is then followed by a list of the alterations caused by the passage of the quarry. Finally, there are confirmatory actions that the tracker can take to gain more evidence.

I will now give some examples to illustrate the attention to detail which is necessary at this stage of the tracker's development. I include a generous list as this is excellent material for use by the tracking instructor.

Example 1   Leaf- and twig-covered area

Natural state:

- Dried twigs, flaking bark, and leaf surfaces will all be aged to the same degree

Disturbed state:

- No actual prints but depressions left
- Twigs squashed, bent and broken
- Freshly broken twigs will be lighter in colour and will have fine fibres left at the ends
- Where bark has been knocked off, the freshly exposed area will be darker and may have a layer of dried powder or granulated debris
- Overturned leaves will expose darker, sand-speckled undersides
- Squashed, crumbled, bent or broken leaves will show the lighter colours of the fresh break, together with the exposed fine hairs of the tear

Confirmatory actions:

- Check bent leaves for flexibility
- Lightly blow on tilted leaves to check their stability
- Study leaves for any transfer deposits – sand or mud
- Feel with the finger tips in any depression for the outline of a print
- Remove leaves from a depression and check for the impression of the print underneath
- Study worm casts under these leaves for evidence of disturbance

Example 2   Leaf- and twig-covered area with growing vegetation

Natural state:

- As above
- No damage to the growing vegetation

Disturbed state:
- As above
- Damage to the growing vegetation including bruising and scraping

Confirmatory actions:
- As above
- Scrutinise any damage for sap evidence
- Make a comparative scrape or damage on an identical plant and note the differences in colour, smell, and viscosity of the fresh sap
- Search for living leaves which have been removed from their parent plant and study these for ageing
- Use any scrapes to assess the direction of movement as well as age

Example 3   Leaf- and twig-covered area with exposed roots
Natural state:
- As for Example 1
- Roots on earth mounds

Disturbed state:
- As for Example 1
- Roots which have been rocked off their earth supports
- Sap flowing from damaged roots
- Imprint of the root adjacent to its original position

Confirmatory actions:
- As for Example 1
- Force the root into the stepped on position to give the direction of travel
- Compare the smell, texture and colour of the sap
- Check the roots for scuff marks

Example 4   Clumps of vegetation interspersed with rocks and stones
Natural state:
- This is usually open country which is exposed to the effects of the elements
- Large patches of clear uniform earth

Disturbed state:
- Prints in the earth
- The earth crust around the sides of the stones and rocks will show signs of disruption

Confirmatory actions:
- Check for prints
- Study the vegetation for damage
- Compare disturbed stones with those in the surrounding area
- Note any deposits of earth on stones and rocks. This when cross-referenced with the time of the last rainfall will give a time bracket

Example 5   Forest floor with a deposit of twigs
Natural state:
- As for Example 1
- Unbroken dead branches and twigs

Disturbed state:
- As for Example 1
- Broken sticks

Confirmatory actions:
- As for Example 1
- Examine the breaks. If the stick is in three parts, that is there are two breaks, it is usually evidence, although not positive proof, that a man has trodden on the stick because of the way humans distribute their weight as they walk
- The centre part which is pushed in the direction of travel is a pointer

Example 6   A stand of saplings
Natural state:
- Trees are upright and parallel

Disturbed state:
- Some plants not in line with the rest

Confirmatory actions:
- Study the leaves on a broken stem to see whether they are still fresh – this gives an indication of the age of the sign
- Inspect the break on the trunk. If the ends are the same colour, then the break is less than seven hours old; if it is an old break, the ends will have died and turned brown

Example 7   Gradients
Natural state:
- Undisturbed

Disturbed state:
  • Prints
Confirmatory actions:
  • Are there slide marks? This is indicative of a tired person who is not confirming his step before transferring his weight
  • Check between the prints for walking stick marks as more information as to the state of the person
  • Examine vegetation which may have been used as a climbing aid. This will give an insight into the morale, fitness, and training of the quarry (fit well-trained troops would not be tempted into this practice because it can easily telegraph their location as the tops of the trees move)
  • Direction of travel can be assessed by the relative depth of the parts of the print (even if the print is not distinctive enough to show a clear heel and toe). A person walking uphill produces a deeper print on the toe as opposed to the heel whilst a person walking down a gradient pushes debris forward of the print

SOME EXERCISES FOR YOUTH LEADERS

Just as there are indoor games which teachers and youth leaders can use to develop the powers of observation, memory, and deduction, there are also games and exercises which are suitable for outdoor use, such as laying trails of varying standards of difficulty and in a variety of scenarios. Also, during walks, whether in the town or the country, the group under training can be quizzed upon items that they have passed. Again, so the habit of observing becomes firmly entrenched, there should be an element of surprise and competition.

The reader involved in training is directed to Chapter Seventeen which is dedicated to the training function.

To emphasise to any group of students the seriousness of the topic, they can be subjected to a more advanced exercise based on the Royal Marine Sniper Test. In this modified practice twelve objects are placed in an arc in front of the observers. The objects are placed up to 300 metres from the observers' position and they are invisible to the naked eye. The students are issued with a copy of a panorama photograph of the arc. With the aid of binoculars the students are then told to observe the arc for forty minutes and plot on to the copy of the photograph and describe the objects. The standard can be adjusted for the age and experience of the group but the Marines fail any student with less than eight out of the twelve – fractional points are deducted for bad plotting, or a poor description.

REPORTING

There is another important factor connected with observation out-of-doors, and that is the necessity for recording in one's mind or on paper exactly what had been observed. A tracker is not much use to others unless he can communicate what he's observed. Your training in observation out-of-doors must of necessity include making reports, making rough sketch-maps and, as your level of expertise advances, making sketches.

CHAPTER EIGHT

Observation of the Individual

One distinct area of observation which is of great relevance to the tracker is the observation of people. This subject is of importance for three main reasons. Firstly, it is an area in which the mental tracking skills of observation, memory, analysis, deduction and comprehension can be practised on a daily basis without any special preparation. Secondly, it concentrates the tracker's mind on the recognisable describable peculiarities of individuals. And thirdly, for the educationalist and those responsible for the development of young people, it has great practical application in the nurturing of the precise use of language which is crucial to the ability to record and report.

MENTAL SKILLS

When travelling and going about his daily business the potential tracker can exercise his skills by noticing every little thing about his fellow passengers and passers-by – their faces, their dress, the way they talk, and any other detail which would help him pass on a description of the individual to someone else.

We have plenty of opportunities to practise and, although we cannot always test the correctness of any deduction we make, it does add more interest both to the observation and the journey if we try and think of the personality and the occupation of the individual.

Judging character from appearances is very difficult and can be very inaccurate but the mental skills which it engages are some of those which a tracker needs to polish to a high level of accomplishment. To reiterate, he observes, remembers, selects and analyses, and then comprehends and deduces.

Apart from the rational application of the mind, the tracker's study of individuals exercises his imagination. It enables him to put himself in the place of another, to live his life, to enter his thoughts. It will be found later on that this is of considerable importance in tracking.

Another interesting aspect of our ability to describe people is that individuals will naturally differ in their point of view and this affects the deductions they make. The story of a doctor is evidence of this. He was able to say that a man had been badly wounded some years previously in his left leg, because he noticed that, when the man was tired, his left shoulder dropped an inch or so lower than his right. The injured man had previously congratulated himself on the fact that no one who did not know could tell of his injury because he had no sign of a limp.

THE DESCRIPTION OF INDIVIDUALS

Judging height and build is important in the observation of individuals and special attention should be paid to these points. Anyone concerned with training beginners will notice that their descriptions pay more attention to the clothes a person is wearing than to the person himself, although it is easier for a person to change his clothes than his height and build. Similarly, a slight change in the facial appearance, such as the absence or addition of a moustache, will guard against a passing scrutiny, whereas a habit of gait or of carriage will give one away at once to a tracker, as these features will usually affect the sign.

To describe an individual with accuracy it is vital to have some scheme with which to break down the task into manageable portions. Also by using a format we ensure that we do not overlook any areas. The following list is a format which breaks down the description into logical sections. It is interesting for the instructor of a group to compare and contrast a group's descriptive efforts before and after being shown this layout.

Format for describing an individual
Sex
Age – in a 5-year bracket. Use their dress, the surroundings, the activity, as well as their physical appearance to assess their age
Height – in a 5-cm bracket. Use reference points – a door is two metres, or compare with a known person
Build – slim, medium, large
Posture – bent, straight, lopsided

Figure 13   Description of facial features

EARS					
Large	Small	Rectangular	Round	Close to head	Protruding
NOSE					
Straight	Convex	Concave	Flat	Pointed	Pug
NOSTRILS					
Horizontal	Turned down	Flaring	Prominent nostrils	Narrow	Wide
MOUTH				Length of upper lip	
Long	Short	Full lips	Straight lips	Long	Short
CHIN					
Round	Square	Pointed	Jutting	Receding	Double
MOUSTACHE					
Long	Short	Handlebar	Turned up ends	Military	Thin
BEARD					
Full	Pointed	Classic	Trendy	Goatee	Designer stubble

Figure 13 continued

Hair – colour, parting, length, style, clean, dirty
Face – complexion, shape, features, facial hair, scars
Eyes – spacing, colour, large, staring, glasses
Gait – speed, stride, limp, swagger, military
Dress – so as to avoid omissions work from the head to the feet
Carrying – describe any articles that the person is holding or carrying
Distinguishing features – if the person has any unusual characteristics note them
Other remarks . . .
Reminds me of . . . If it is possible, name a person to whom the individual has a likeness

One of the hardest parts of the person to describe but one of the best recognition features is the person's face. To overcome this problem it is very useful to use the breakdown of facial features in figure 13.

LANGUAGE SKILLS

As was stated in the Introduction, I also hope this book will help people who have responsibilities for the personal development of the young. It is to this aim that I address the following points. To be able to describe accurately and briefly demands the exercise and command of strong powers of expression. Therefore the practice of describing individuals can only help the communication skills of young people. To this end I again would draw your attention to how much detail can be given about a person's face by a good command of the language and a logical approach as is demonstrated by the drawings and descriptions in figure 13.

Finally, I would like to suggest some games which can also be of use in training the powers of observing people. Again, these will be found to be of great assistance to the youth leader.

GAMES FOR OBSERVATION

Dressing statues   A person is arranged by one group in a pose and wearing specific items of dress. The second group then enter the room and are allowed two minutes to observe the figure. They then depart and the figure resumes his normal dress and position. The group then re-enter and have three to five minutes to rearrange the figure as they first saw it.

The unrehearsed incident   During an unrelated activity a pre-determined incident is enacted. The incident should be dramatic and brief. The observers are then tested on what they can remember of the events. It will amaze them that the same events can be remembered in so many different ways. The use of a video of the original incident can be very informative in that it will exhibit beyond any doubt what actually took place.

From 'go' to 'stop'   In this game the participants are to observe every action of a particular person from the word 'go' to the word 'stop'. The person selected need only go through a few more or less ordinary actions such as lighting a cigarette and walking a few paces. As the skills of the group progress the actions can become more complicated and the time extended.

GAMES TO EXERCISE THE POWERS OF DEDUCTION
AND IMAGINATION

Empty your pockets   A number of small articles, such as are carried in a man's pockets – a matchbox, a pen, a few coins, an old receipt, the return half of a railway ticket, a small note book and so on – are placed on a tray or table. A story is told of a man being found wandering about having lost his memory or of a man being found unconscious or dead. You are to try to identify him if possible, or give some useful guide as to his identification from the contents of his pockets. Naturally, the instructor needs to expend considerable thought in preparation so that the items from the pockets are compatible with the suggested answer.

Dressing up   The important part of a disguise is not so much dressing the part, that is comparatively easy, but acting the part. That is one of the reasons why play-acting is of undoubted use in persuading people to use their imagination and to try and get into the skin of the person they are following.

CHAPTER NINE

The Principles of Stalking

I realise that the word stalking nowadays has ugly connotations but I do not apologise for using it in this chapter. It is simply a word which has been misused to label an unsavoury activity. The criminal/pest stalker gets his strange thrills from the victim knowing of his existence, whereas the stalker's quarry in a hunt should never be aware of the tracker/stalker. Therefore I will continue to use the word with the meaning it has had for several hundred years.

We are now aware of the importance to the tracker of acute powers of observation. The serious student of tracking will now realise, having read the previous chapters on sign, what can be accomplished with well-practised skills of observation.

The next logical step along the trail of acquiring skills for tracking is to gain an appreciation of stalking. The following military tracking scenario will demonstrate how relevant stalking is to the life of the tracker.

I purposely used the expression 'to the life of the tracker' because to the military tracker that is what is at stake – his life. As the sign gets fresher and the trail hotter, so does the danger as the tracker closes with his quarry – the enemy. Man is more dangerous than the big game animals according to many SAS jungle soldiers, being more aggressive, better armed, and more cunning than any of the big five trophies collected by the mollycoddled, safari hunter – lion, tiger, rhino, buffalo and elephant.

So, just as observation is an essential for the tracker to be able to detect the sign as he gets near his quarry, it is equally essential that he practises the skills of the stalker. This is as true for the conservationist, the ornithologist, the deer hunter, as it is for the soldier. I have decided to place stalking before other chapters which deal with elements of tracking proper because it is another of the building blocks without which tracking proper is only half appreciated.

Also, for the outdoor pursuits instructor the stalking exercise described at the end of the next chapter is far easier to administer and control than a tracking exercise. But the practice and the playing of stalking exercises will undoubtedly make the individual eager to go on to tracking.

Personally, I hold that it is necessary that every potential tracker should learn the main principles of stalking before he can practise tracking in its wider sense.

WHAT IS STALKING?

It is the art of approaching an object under cover or by stealth. It is more generally described as the ability to move rapidly, or fairly rapidly, from place to place, without being seen, heard, or otherwise detected, whilst at the same time seeing and observing.

Therefore, there are two aspects to stalking. The first is the concealment of the stalker. The second is the movement of the stalker. These two points are, of course, closely interrelated and interdependent.

CAMOUFLAGE

The living natural world gives the astute student of tracking many important guidelines. Out in the countryside you rarely see birds and animals standing out against trees and bushes, they usually offer an indistinct outline, in or behind a bush. The camouflage of animals and birds is a subject in itself, a full study of which is beyond the scope of this book. What matters to us here is the principle of concealment.

The aim of the stalker should be to blend in with the background, remembering the reasons why things are seen: shape, shadow, shine, silhouette, spacing and movement.

The first consideration for the tracker/stalker is the choice of clothing. The colour of the material is very important. Colours should be of neutral tones – not too light or too dark. The colour should not be uniform, as this helps to give shape to the person – an aspect which the stalker is trying to disguise. A ghillie suit (a camouflage suit to which has been added different coloured strips of hessian and netting), is a prime example of how the shape of clothing can be altered to hide the shape of the person.

Often dark clothing with a top up of local vegetation, combined with clever, well thought out movements, is better than military camouflage worn by someone who thinks that the jacket itself makes him invisible and proceeds in a lazy, slapdash way. A camouflage jacket is not enough on its own. In fact military camouflage is designed for specific theatres of operation – the jungle, desert, arctic – and if worn out of context, is more of a hindrance than a help.

Clothing and skin can be darkened by smearing mud on it but make sure that when dry it doesn't lighten too much. Another aid to personal camouflage is charcoal.

Nature gives some very good guidelines for the design and use of camouflage even to the extent that the under parts of birds and animals tend to be of a considerably lighter shade than their upper parts so that, whether viewed from above against the ground or from below against the sky, they still blend in. Aircraft camouflage tends to use this principle.

The colour of the material is but one aspect. The outline shape which the camouflage lends to the stalker is of equal importance.

As the stalker moves through the countryside, especially the open countryside, he should continually monitor the changes in vegetation and adjust his camouflage as necessary by adding vegetation from the surrounding area. In forested and urban areas the addition of camouflage is used less. Here the use of shadow and the avoidance of shine and silhouette become much more important.

CONCEALMENT

The stalker will always be aware of his background. He will move position in order to place himself against a backdrop which conceals him. It is not necessary always to conceal yourself behind cover. The backdrop is just as important and in fact observing from behind cover if done incorrectly can lead to the discovery of the stalker far more quickly than being in front of the appropriate backdrop – see figure 14.

The tracker should always be aware of being skylined. Apart from the obvious skyline, there are equally important intermediate skylines of which the tracker and stalker must be conscious.

Don't look different from your surroundings

Wear appropriate clothing

Blend in

Don't shine

Avoid skylines (Silhouette)

Lose your shape

Figure 14   The art of concealment

If carrying anything which shines, such as binoculars, camera, compass, or if you are wearing a watch or a ring, ensure that it is covered from the sun otherwise it will point to the wearer's position like a flashing mirror. It is a point that is often overlooked, but some clothing becomes shiny when wet.

KNOWLEDGE OF THE QUARRY

It is also a principle of stalking that you know as much as possible about your quarry. It is a mistake to underestimate it. The following is a list of useful questions about the quarry which the stalker should try and answer:

- How does it feed?
- Where does it feed?
- What precautions does it take to guard against surprise?
- How quick is it to take alarm?
- What sort of place does it frequent?
- What kind of cover does it go to?
- How does it get there?

When you have observed, analysed, and understood, you are then ready to solve the problem of the final approach to the quarry.

It is vitally important for the military tracker and the big game tracker to have as deep a knowledge as possible of the quarry, because of the threat it poses. Big game hunters will confirm the theory that it is possible to train up to a pitch where one becomes aware of impending danger. The development of this sense is necessary for the visual tracker. It is possible to be alert and efficient but relaxed, only becoming attuned and aware of danger when it is life-threatening. A tracker living every moment on his nerves while on a track will burn up too much nervous energy and will not last. This sort of experience, which almost gives a tracker a sixth sense, cannot be gained from books however detailed. This level of field craft can only be gained by practice and having the good fortune to accompany experienced trackers.

In the isolated areas of many countries, the native bird, insect and animal life have their own way of warning fellow creatures of danger from predators or intruders. Some examples will make this clear:

- The blackbird in the English hedgerow will soon realise the intentions of the small boy with his sling shot, and as it flies off, will give its loud warning cry alerting all the wildlife in the area
- The plover, which is often seen in Kenya near the basking crocodile, will hover over a stalking man, giving its warning cry
- The barking deer will shout to all in the area at the approach of a tiger or man in India
- Monkeys in the Far East not only shout to all around of man's presence, but I have known them to throw sticks down at you from the tree tops
- A startled pheasant will cry its warning to the rest of the animal kingdom
- The domestic dog will bark its warning of the presence of a stranger
- Wild fish will dart away into deeper water when startled, warning others of a potential danger

- Often insects will warn of any intruder into the area by their silence

These are but a few of the cases where the wildlife may warn the tracker of possible dangers near by or, alternately, warn the quarry of the tracker's presence.

First-hand knowledge of the habits and nature of the wild life in any new area must be known and used to the tracker's advantage. Many a time during my trips to the jungle, if the breeze was blowing in our faces oncoming pigs would walk right past the patrol. I knew that the pigs were partially deaf and blind but that they have an acute sense of smell. So to avoid them alerting the rest of the jungle by rushing off once they smelt us, we would move quietly off to one side and they would pass unconcernedly on their way.

THE WIND

The wind is one of the stalker's greatest difficulties, and nothing but long practice will enable you to understand it completely. But it is very important to start to take this element into account, especially if your quarry has a well-developed sense of smell.

The tracker/stalker must also take into account the effect the wind has on the carriage of sound. Sometimes it has an adverse effect and sounds carry towards the quarry, whereas at other times the noise generated by the wind can cover the sound of your movements.

Again we can see how important it is for the tracker to get into the skin of his quarry – he must try and think like his quarry so that he can outfox him. He must know the strengths and weaknesses of the animal whose spoor he is following. I remember the Highland ghillies telling me as a boy that the red deer can not only see and hear you at a thousand yards, but that they can also smell you at that distance if you were foolish enough to be windward of them.

As you develop your tracking skills you will start to realise that no one factor can be taken in isolation and this is just as true of the wind as any other feature in the tracker's world. The movement of air is affected by the topography of the area and the whole world of scent is affected by temperature and humidity because these factors affect the rate of evaporation.

The interaction of relief and airflow is very relevant to the stalker. On level ground the wind does not vary very much without warning whilst a wind blowing uphill or along the side of a hill is usually steadier by far than one blowing downhill. The tracker has to bear in mind that strong smells will be carried for some distance by even the lightest wind before dispersing, and that any smell will tend to settle in low-lying areas and will linger in still air.

It is easy to find out the actual direction of the wind by wetting a finger and holding it up. The coolest is the direction from which the wind is blowing. Or you can throw up a pinch of dried vegetation to check the direction if it is a light breeze. If the wind is stronger the movement of the trees and bushes will indicate the direction. Again another good indicator of the strength and direction of the wind is the movement of the clouds, but be aware that the higher clouds may be moving in a slightly different direction to those at a lower altitude.

Animals respond to the warning received by their noses far more quickly than by their sight or hearing. Unless you approach an animal with the wind, or even a breeze, blowing in from the animal to you it is doubtful if you will get very close before it flees. In fact, your scent may so effectively advertise your presence that you may not even see an animal which has moved quickly away. If the wind direction is unfavourable when you first sight your quarry it is best to make your way in a wide circle around the quarry until you are in a more favourable position from which to move forward.

As with all the features a tracker observes, he doesn't merely note the wind and record it but he continually monitors its changes. There is probably no feature of the environment that can change so quickly to the disadvantage to the tracker and stalker as the wind.

One moment the deer herd is upwind to you. They gradually shift their location as they graze the hillside and before you realise you are obliquely upwind to them – disaster! It will only be seconds before their scent sentries have you on their radar and the alarm will go up.

SCENT

As well as being conscious of how your quarry reacts you must objectively study yourself. Don't forget that the human stinks to many animals. The world seen through the eyes of a dog is one of scent which leaves a trail which can be more permanent to the dog than visual sign is to the tracker. Your pet dog's mental map of your neighbourhood would give a very different and enlightening view of the streets. It would be as astonishing as when you first see a thermal imaging camera showing up the heat loss of an uninsulated house.

The tracker has to be aware of the scent that he may be giving out which will alert his quarry whether it be human or animal. To eliminate any possible chance of the quarry detecting you by smell it may be necessary to avoid any of the following for two or three days before going on a tracking task:

- Toothpaste
- After-shave lotion, scents and deodorants
- Soap
- Hair gel
- Talcum powder
- Shaving soap
- Shampoo
- Medications such as liniments
- Spices such as garlic

Whilst you are on a tracking operation it may be necessary to use only cold food.

Clothing can be given an acceptable smell by hanging it up on the clothes line to weather for a few days or hanging it up anywhere away from characteristic clinging smells. I would not recommend any other method, like burying your equipment or hanging your equipment over a fire, as this will only make you smell like a ploughed field or a burnt out fire and the quarry will be alerted.

The following are some of the scents that the students may come across in their tracking exercises:

- Animal and human latrines
- Animal scent posts
- Animal homes – earths, setts, dens, and burrows
- Animal scent glands
- Dead animals
- Cooking fumes
- Smoke, burnt wood
- Newly dug earth

In addition, the visual tracker, especially the military tracker, must use his sense of smell to warn him of any danger. The following would alert a soldier on a tracking mission:

- Cooking smells
- Human sanitation
- Domesticated animal smells
- Camp fires
- Slaughtered animals
- Freshly dug earth

Distinctive animal odours are dependent on the diet, and humans whose primary food is meat will smell differently to those whose diet is vegetarian. The diet of different races makes each one smell differently, as any jungle soldier will tell you.

SMOKING

At this point I would like to touch on smoking. It is very difficult to give up smoking, but I do believe that if you are going to treat tracking seriously you should attempt to do so. Certainly, you should not smoke whilst on a tracking task and, if possible, a couple of days before going on a tracking task.

Smoking can:

- Affect your sense of smell
- Give away your position by the smell, the cloud of smoke, cigarette waste such as butts and ash, and by a smoker's cough
- Reduce your concentration because of your concern about the next cigarette rather than the tracking task

Tracking and stalking can be seen as points on a continuum where one shades into the other, depending upon the closeness of the quarry or the enemy. Now that we have firmly established stalking within the tracking context we will move on, in the next chapter, to the practical aspects of stalking.

CHAPTER TEN

Stalking Techniques

After successfully following the sign for several kilometres, or in some military situations, several days, it would be frustrating and probably very dangerous to alert the quarry to your presence before you were ready. To that end this chapter will demonstrate the practical expertise which the tracker has to gain so that he can covertly approach his quarry in the final stages of the pursuit.

Stalking is no longer natural to us – it needs the study and practice of techniques. The actual practice is often difficult and uncomfortable as you crawl across rough ground and through tangled spiky vegetation.

THE TRACKER/STALKER'S PROGRESS
The actual methods of movement available to the stalker approaching his quarry will be described in detail later in this chapter.

The type of cover which a stalker has to contend with can be very scant or non-existent but, by judicious route-planning, he will make use of every crease and fold in the ground to approach his quarry. This approach will probably not be direct because it is following the best cover. With practice it is possible to move at a reasonable speed in comparative silence – move steadily and carefully.

As the tracker/stalker moves, his gaze continually sweeps far and near, right and left, up and down, looking not only at bushes and trees but through and beyond them – he disregards the general pattern of foliage. The untrained stalker usually looks at a bush, failing to see what is behind or in it.

The tracker is conscious that completely new arcs of visibility are opening up in which the quarry may be waiting. To inspect the ground the tracker stops, goes down on one knee, waits for the cover man if he is a military tracker, and only then lowers his head to look at the ground. Whether the tracker is stationary or moving, only his eyes are ever directed towards the ground. He doesn't lower his head in order to look at the sign and this is especially important whilst he is moving forward.

He crouches down occasionally, as this often provides a better view through the vegetation, especially in what is termed close country such as you find in secondary jungle.

When working through woods and undergrowth don't brush through the small bushes but slowly lift them aside with your hand and then ease them back into place – don't let them spring back. This technique not only cuts out a great deal of noise but also it eliminates unnecessary movement of the vegetation. Do not grab branches, saplings or bushes for extra support, leverage, or balance, when crossing an obstacle, getting up off the ground, or when climbing a hill because the slightest movement at the base is magnified at the top. This movement will give your position away. Flag-waving or telegraphing is the term given to this phenomenon and remember the message is transmitted in all directions not just forwards. Avoid treading on dry leaves, sticks or rotten wood. Don't allow yourself to become caught up in vines or overhanging creepers and, if you are, remove any spiky trailing fronds carefully and silently from your clothing.

If you think you have been spotted or you have been caught out in the open, remain perfectly still, freeze, until your quarry turns its head away. Then move slowly and quietly back into cover. Even when right out in the open there is no cause for alarm, provided your background harmonises with your clothes, and you remain perfectly motionless. You will certainly arouse suspicion, and probably alarm, if you disappear suddenly. The only time when rapid movement back into cover is recommended is when it is a human who has surprised you and even then circumstances will dictate whether to freeze or flee, but if you move any other animal will instantly be put to flight.

There is a specific technique to freezing which again I will describe later.

Generally speaking, in stalking try to avoid working with the sun in your face, especially when the sun is low on the horizon in the morning or in the evening. There are several reasons for this. Firstly, it is difficult to distinguish an object in the distance with the sun in your eyes. Secondly, it is easier for the quarry to spot you with the sun shining on your clothes. Unfortunately, this is a natural paradox which you will soon become aware of, as you realise that it is easier to make out a track with the sun shining towards you casting a shadow on the track.

LISTENING HALTS

As the tracker approaches his quarry and the skills of stalking come into play it is essential to take listening halts. You and your team should not make any noise which will travel beyond the distance which you can see – otherwise the quarry or enemy may be aware of you before you see them.

Listening halts should be taken frequently. The tracker and his team should remain perfectly still and position themselves low down in shadow or shade, and against an appropriate background, otherwise the slightest movement on your part will attract attention.

To listen most effectively it is necessary to cock your head in the direction of where you are listening, and to open your mouth slightly as this aids the working of the hearing mechanism.

STALKING SKILLS

If one word should be remembered by a stalker it is – stealthily. This word exactly describes the mode of progress that should be adopted. The actual method, walking, crawling or slithering, varies according to the distance you are from your quarry and the kind of country you are moving through, but all the time you must use cunning and move stealthily.

I will now detail the different methods used by the tracker on his final approach – the stalk.

THE CAUTIOUS APPROACH

This merely consists in walking calmly and quietly in the direction of the supposed quarry or in a direction which you consider is favourable to your purpose, having taken into account all aspects of the environment, including the terrain, obstacles and the wind direction. You have not come to grips with the quarry yet, but there is no knowing when you may come to close quarters and so you have to be wary and take advantage of rising ground, of dips, of the cover afforded by trees and bushes, or the bed of a stream. Even this requires practice and an eye for ground, so that any casual observation does not lead you along a wrong line which will suddenly expose you to the view of everybody and everything within miles.

THE UPRIGHT CROUCH

When you are getting within range, your approach must be made still more cautiously. It is best to adopt what is usually known as the upright crouching position – see figure 15. This requires practice in lifting the feet and in balance. The feet should point straight forward to offer the least resistance to any obstacles that may be encountered. If the toes turn out they act as hooks. The knees should be kept slightly bent and relaxed. The feet should be lifted well off the ground at every step, and not shuffled along.

Walk slowly and watch the placement of your feet. Tread on the outside of your foot first and roll your foot on and off the ground, be ready to withdraw the foot should it come into contact with anything which is likely to make noise. The ball of the foot should touch the ground first, followed by the heel. The weight of the body should be placed gradually on the sole of the

Figure 15 The upright crouch

foot to avoid snapping any twig that may be underneath it, or kicking any stones. A firm balance should be obtained on each leg in turn before the other is advanced, so that at any moment, in any place, and in any position, you can remain poised like a statue, and as quiet. At the same time the arms should be kept still as you move and not be swung about violently.

Every movement should be stealthy, silent and deliberate. In fact, you must put your brain into the sole of your feet and your eyes into your toes as you feel your way along. The best place to start to practise is a small wood or coppice which is strewn with dry leaves and sticks. So you will feel the ground better try thin-soled shoes, or just thick socks and, depending on the surface and your feet, you can even try stalking barefoot to achieve even greater sensitivity.

THE FELINE CRAWL

When the distance between you and your quarry is lessening and when cover is getting scarce it will be necessary to employ the feline crawl – see figure 16. Any common domestic cat can demonstrate this method to you. Watch a cat, study its methods and copy them – the cat family are probably the greatest exponents of stalking. The hind paw comes automatically up to the position that the corresponding front paw has occupied. You have to crawl along on hands and knees. The hands feel for suitable places on which to rest and the corresponding knee comes up to the same position. Care should be taken to lift the knee and foot from the ground and not to drag them, but equal care should be exercised so that the feet are not waved in the air.

Figure 16   The feline crawl

Also do not hump the body up in the middle like a camel, keep the hindquarters low. The head should be the highest part, and that, too, should be kept as low as possible, and certainly not bobbed up suddenly or jerked from side to side. As before, every movement that is made should be slow and deliberate.

THE FLAT OR BELLY CRAWL

Lastly, there is the flat crawl – see figure 17. This procedure is used for the final stage of the stalk. It is slow and very tiring, especially for the abdominal muscles. It is necessary to go down full length on the ground, flat on the abdomen, with the head down. The body and legs should be kept stiff and the legs close together. The toes should be turned well out and the heels kept down so that practically the whole of the inner side of the foot rests upon the ground. If this is not done consciously, there is a tendency for the feet to come up and attract attention. You now have to work yourself forward, bit by bit, a few inches at a time, using the hands and the sides of the feet. This can be done by placing your forearm flat on the ground in front of your head and by bringing the other forearm up in front of it, and so on, the toes being used as levers on which to work. Instead of using the forearms it is possible to move forward by placing the hands on the ground close to, almost under, the body on a level with the chest, and pulling yourself forward with them. Care should be taken to keep the elbows well down and close to the sides.

If it is safe to expose the head sufficiently to look round, then it is possible to do the flat crawl more on the side than on the stomach, and to bend the knees sideways and bring them up to

Figure 17   The flat crawl

help. Your movements will then be something of a cross between a feline crawl and a flat crawl.

With all methods of movement the stalker must be aware of the vegetation above and around him. If he is not careful with his movements the grass and bushes will telegraph his progress towards the quarry.

FREEZING

Frequently you find that when you are stalking, even when going dead slow, you suddenly burst out of cover and are liable to be spotted. In that case there is only one thing to do. You must freeze instantaneously, and when the opportunity offers slowly and carefully work back to cover again, remembering that any sudden movement is liable to give you away.

In these circumstances, it is best to crawl backwards, keeping your body and legs stiff, and levering yourself back with your toes and hands working together. At the same time your face and hands should be kept close to the ground and steady. Even when you are back in cover again, be very cautious about raising your head.

The art of freezing was touched upon in the previous chapter. It is not necessary that you should be behind something to remain unobserved. If there is a suitable background it is possible to assume a position right out in the open without any danger of being noticed, provided you keep your body, limbs, and especially your head still. This technique needs a good deal of practice so that whatever method of stalking you are using, you can instantly become still and then remain motionless for a considerable period. Although this technique is most effective with a non-human quarry it has its place in the repertoire of skills to be used when stalking a human, although then the background, distance and light conditions are more critical.

Canadian hunters lay great emphasis on the best pose to adopt when freezing during a stalk. They not only remain motionless, but they adopt a pose which reflects the character of the surrounding trees, bushes and rocks. So that amongst perfectly straight trees they would stand erect, whereas if they were in an area with many uprooted trees they would adopt a more irregular pose by bending and twisting their body and arms. Obviously they slowly and cautiously take up these shapes, they don't snap into them.

LYING STILL

The practice of lying or sitting perfectly still, during the day or at night, and letting the wildlife in an area become used to your presence enables you to learn a great deal about what is happening. The novice will be amazed how the wildlife starts to return and totally ignore you if you stay still for a long period. I've been fortunate enough to see some remarkable sights as I've lain perfectly motionless for hours in observation or sentry positions – vibrantly coloured humming birds within arms length beating their wings at a rate which defies the eyes as they hover to draw out the nectar from jungle flowers; vixens bringing out their cubs to play by the safety of the den entrance.

A sophisticated version of this habit takes place on the hide which the bird photographer constructs. The detailed subject of hides is beyond the scope of this book. But it should be noted by the serious student of tracking that a hide acts as a good observation post for any individual who desires to study nature.

Tree hides can also be effective, provided the observer realises he is not hidden when he sits across a branch. You must conform to the lines of the tree.

ROUTE-PLANNING

Apart from the techniques of moving silently and covertly there is another very pertinent subject which is often overlooked entirely by the amateur and that is route-planning and selection, see figure 18. Military snipers when they are given a target to stalk are also issued with aerial photography and stereoscopes so that they can plan the approach to the enemy with meticulous precision. Chapter Twenty is devoted in its entirety to the associated skills of map-reading.

The route will seldom be the most direct but the experienced tracker will take all the following points into consideration before embarking on the final stage of the pursuit.

WIND DIRECTION AND STRENGTH

As we know the wind not only carries smell but sound and therefore you should stalk with the wind in your face.

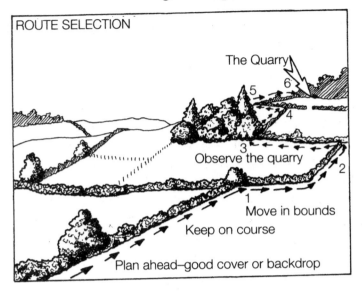

Figure 18   Route selection for the stalker

VEGETATION

As the vegetation cover alters, so the stalker has to select new material to top up his personal camouflage.

MOVEMENT

Each leg of the stalk will probably require a different method of movement. For instance, if you are behind a hedgerow and not visible from the quarry a crouching posture will be ideal, whereas if you are working your way through a wheat field which is overlooked by the quarry it will be necessary to adopt the feline crawl.

LANDMARKS

During the stalk you will require reference points for orientation purposes. These must be visible without exposing yourself, for example pylons, trees, high ground, and the sun, moon and stars.

COVER

Check that the obvious features, such as ditches, walls, hedges, buildings, river beds will actually cover you to your destination and that the cover is complete – many hedgerows have gaps in them and ditches terminate abruptly in impassably small drainage pipes.

DEAD GROUND

This is a military term which is used to describe an area which, although overlooked by an observer, is a blind spot to him because of the folds in the ground. It is of great importance to the stalker, as he can move through such areas with impunity because he is out of sight. To the inexperienced stalker it can be unnerving moving in dead ground in open country, as he feels completely exposed, but it is far safer than following a broken hedgerow in full sight of the target. Of course, in certain circumstances you may have to consider the wind and scent.

OBSTACLES

The route-planning has to take into account any obstacles before the stalker sets off. He should have a good idea in his mind as to how he will overcome each and every obstacle. A prime consideration in obstacle crossing is skylining – avoid it but if it is unavoidable do it briefly and keep as low as possible and, for example, roll away from the crest of a hill.

ROADS

Try and plan to cross these at bends or corners.

PLOUGHED LAND

Use the furrows as cover.

LONG GRASS OR CEREAL CROPS

Keep changing direction so that there isn't a uniform predictable movement of the foliage.

OBSERVATION POINTS

There should be pre-planned points at which you will halt and observe the quarry. This is necessary in case the animal has moved or the human quarry is planning any actions which could affect you. It is imperative that you can see without being seen, so pick observation points that allow you to look through cover rather than over it.

NOISE

The stalker has to take advantage of existing noises, such as streams, wind, rain, vehicles, the sea, or aircraft to cover any sounds that he may make. He should ensure that the contents of his pockets and any equipment that he is carrying does not make any sound that will carry. Before a stalk this can easily be checked by jumping up and down a few times. The stalker selects his clothing with the elimination of noise in mind because many fabrics, especially waterproof ones, rustle when in contact with vegetation. Watches that chime or beep should be left behind, along with pagers, mini cassette recorders and mobile phones. Remember that sound travels in all directions. Visibility in close country can be very limited, so the visual tracker must ensure that sounds made will not travel beyond the distance he can see. Thus he will avoid alerting an unsuspecting quarry of his approach. Silence is essential at all times. All extraneous noise has to be excluded – this refers both to voice and movement. Because the tracker has to eliminate all sounds, military trackers have developed a series of hand signals for communicating within their group – see below.

ANIMALS

As previously mentioned, any wildlife that you disturb will alert the quarry and the curiosity of domesticated animals will, apart from the more obvious barking of dogs, be noticed by the observant enemy.

HILLSIDES

If you are stalking on a mountain or hillside, try to put yourself into a position above the quarry but avoid skylining. Animals tend to look for danger coming from below. On mountains the stalker has to avoid displacing rocks.

STALKING ANIMALS

Grazing animals tend to raise their heads at frequent but irregular intervals, so do not be tempted to make a sudden dash or any quick movement, as you can be caught out and they will be put to flight.

ALTERNATIVE ROUTES

After choosing the main route, consider other paths in case you have to abort or modify the stalk for reasons such as a change in the wind direction, movement of the quarry, or third party interference.

HAND SIGNALS

The hand signals which military trackers use are a refinement of the infantry hand signals. Such is their importance that trackers always rehearse them immediately before a patrol. The group may have its own variations relevant to that particular theatre of operations. The numbers of silent hand signals are kept to a minimum so as to avoid confusion – remember these are being used to communicate vital, perhaps life-saving information, at a time when the patrol is within hearing distance of the enemy. See figure 19 for some of the more common hand signals used.

THE TRACKING/STALKING GROUP

The tracker has to be aware that he must control the group that he is with. He either does this himself or the commander of the group is mindful of the tracker's work and he manages this role. The party has to be controlled for the following reasons:
- Silence is paramount
- Preservation of the sign – the tracker's group must not inadvertently spoil the sign

EXERCISES AND PRACTICES FOR THE INSTRUCTOR

Stalking is usually associated with the wilds, with big game hunting, and with deer stalking. But it is not necessary to have something very large to stalk. You can get a great deal of good experience stalking a dog, a cat, or any of the smaller wild animals, such as rabbits.

Before students are asked to undertake a stalk they should be well practised in adopting the different stalking positions and in moving across the ground by the different methods. These preparatory drills should include, at intervals, the instruction to freeze.

Now we are able to undertake a full scale stalking practice. To emphasise the seriousness of stalking the students can be told

Figure 19 Hand signals for the stalker/tracker

that this exercise is based upon a test which military snipers have to undertake.

For the instructor all that is required for this exercise is an observer or two with binoculars, controllers who walk near the students who are carrying out the stalk, a suitable piece of land which is either private or where there are not likely to be any disturbances from other groups, and communications between the observer and the controllers.

The students are briefed to the effect that they have:

- A start point – about 1000 metres from the observer
- Boundaries to the area in which they can move
- To get within 150–200 metres of the observer – rough limits should be outlined by the controller as to the extent of this bracket
- That they must be in a position to observe the quarry from their chosen position
- A time limit – approximately 45–60 minutes

The students then attempt to accomplish the task. The controllers stay within sight of the stalkers but as far from them as possible. It is best if there is a controller to each stalker as the stalkers may take very different routes to the target. When the observers think they have seen any of the stalkers they radio the controllers and direct them to where they think there is a stalker. The controller does not aid the observer or the stalker. When the student is in position he declares it to the nearest controller. The controller then moves within ten metres of the stalker and tells the observer that he has three minutes to locate the stalker. If he is unsuccessful the controller moves to within five metres and the procedure is repeated – and then finally to within arm's length.

The outdoor pursuits instructor can ring the changes for the students by letting them be observers and controllers in turn so as to see the problems from another standpoint.

The type of terrain chosen is a very important consideration. So as not to discourage the student in the early stages the mission should be achievable. As the group's level of expertise increases the stalking problems can be made more difficult.

In the debriefs they will soon realise the golden rule of stalking: you take your risks early in a stalk, when the target is further away. As a rule, the nearer you are to the quarry the lower and slower you need to be.

The stalking practice above will impress upon the tracking student the patience, planning, and skill required to carry out a successful stalk.

To summarise:

- Routes must be planned
- Avoid impassable obstacles – marshes, open ground
- Move in bounds from observation position to observation position
- Keep a check on your course
- Observe without being seen
- Remember . . .

The golden rule of stalking
take
risks
early

CHAPTER ELEVEN

Night Movement

Because of the huge differences in the methods which have to be used at night compared to those that we use in the day the subject deserves a chapter to itself.

The major difference is the switch in emphasis away from sight to hearing, touch and smell. Even when the ambient noise level is the same at night as during the day one's hearing seems to be more acute. It is as if the senses are compensating for each other.

The importance of the other senses compensating for each other when the visibility is poor is well illustrated by the experience of a friend of mine. He wasn't tracking but he was the lead scout in a patrol in an enemy stronghold during the Dhofar War in the early 'seventies. The patrol was operating in very close country and the monsoon mist was like a heavy shroud over the scrub, especially during the first light period just before dawn. He was able to alert the rest of the patrol to the presence of the enemy because he detected the smell of camel meat being boiled over an open wood fire. It was the adoo (the enemy) preparing their breakfast. Although they were still involved in a heavy fire fight, things could have been a great deal worse without that moment's forewarning.

The sense of smell is an aid not only to discover your quarry but also to fix your whereabouts if you are in known country. Smoke, whether of tobacco or of a fire, can be smelt at incredibly long distances at night.

NIGHT VISION

We can see in the dark.

The retina of the eye is made up of light-sensitive cells. These are either cone-shaped or rod-shaped. The rods provide us with our night vision. They only distinguish between black and white and they have a reaction time before they are fully effective. If you walk from a lit room into the night, you know how you find yourself temporarily blind. This is while the change over from cones to rods takes place. Full night vision takes about forty minutes to come into operation. However, the process is a gradual one. The rods adapt very quickly at first and then slow down gradually, so you have most of your night vision within the first five to ten minutes.

Observe the effects of night vision for yourself. Walk from a well-lit situation into the darkness outside. At first you will see nothing, but you will be aware of a red tint to the darkness. After only a few seconds the outline of larger objects will be visible and the details on those objects will begin to show after a few more minutes. After ten minutes the detail on the faces of people around you will be easily recognisable and you may also be able to recognise larger individual plants at ground level. To pick out distant detail at night, flick your eyes on and off the object or look slightly to one side of it. The one major problem with night vision is that it is instantly lost as soon as a light shines into your eyes. To get night vision back you must go through the forty-minutes process once more. There are a few things we can do to avoid losing night vision. If you sense a light is about to shine in your eyes, simply close them. If you need to make use of that light, but still retain night vision, close just one eye. Night vision will be preserved in the eye which was kept closed, although you will be left with a strange lopsided feel to your vision for a few minutes.

When a torch or several torches are to be used, ensure the torch-carriers are aware of night vision and the effect that light has on it. Get them to shine torches at the ground, not in the air or in people's faces. Try, as much as possible, to avoid using torches at night – they only illuminate a short distance in front of you, whereas night vision will reach the horizon and so is far more suitable for observation or navigation purposes. A group of people walking at night, all with torches switched on, will be walking in a bubble of light. The immediate ground around will be well lit, but the eyes will not be able to penetrate beyond the bubble.

One compromise is to use red or green filters on torches to help preserve your night vision.

To summarise, at night:

- We see less than in daylight
- We see shapes not detail
- We see skylines and silhouettes
- We may see movement
- If caught in the light of a vehicle, freeze, quickly close one eye to protect your night vision
- Use night vision aids if available

DIRECTION FINDING

Loss of sight brings with it loss of direction – people eventually walk in a kind of spiral, and one often hears of people lost in the jungle or in mist coming back on their own track.To remedy this inevitable tendency it is necessary to take precautions when you start on your night stalk.

If it is a clear starlit night you will experience no difficulty, as the stars will give you your direction, provided you take your bearings when you start.

There may be a slightly stronger light in the west, or in the east, depending on the time of night, which will give you a rough indication of direction.

Even in the dark, try to make a note of the landmarks that you pass, taking care to glance back at them after you have passed so that you will recognise the differences in their appearance from the other side.

If there are no stars to guide you, your difficulties are increased. The wind may help, if it is constant, and if you note its direction at the start.

At night, when there is stillness in the air, a man's voice, the bark of a dog, or the rumble of a train, will carry a long distance compared with these same sounds by day. This can be a guide to the direction if you have sufficient local knowledge.

Sounds carry through the ground, so if you place your ear to the ground, or against the end of a stick that is touching the ground, you can frequently hear footsteps a long way off. If it is difficult to identify the exact quarter from which a sound comes, it is a help to block one ear.

NOISE

On the other hand, the noises that you make will be correspondingly intensified and so it behoves you to be very careful as you move. At first you will find that you are certain to make more noise as you night stalk, in which case do what you can to move only when there is covering noise in existence, such as the wind in the trees or, if you are in heavily populated country, the noise of a motor car passing down an adjacent road.

BALANCE

The methods of movement you utilise are basically the same as those used in the day (see Movement at Night below), but you will find it more difficult to keep your balance. Because of this you will find the obstacles more difficult to negotiate. If you want to carry out a simple experiment to prove how losing the sense of sight disturbs the power of balance, stand on tiptoe and, still standing on tiptoe, shut your eyes. Almost immediately you will discover a tendency to overbalance – probably forwards.

SKYLINING

It is best to keep as low down as possible. The dangers of the skyline have been referred to before but it is especially grave at night.

SHADOWS

During night stalking, shadows can be just as much a danger as an advantage. The stalker can use the shadow to conceal his presence but on the other hand he has to be aware of letting his own shadow fall on a lit patch of ground – see Chapter Seven for a full explanation of the effects of shadow.

MOVEMENT AT NIGHT

Daylight movements are not suitable at night, they have to be adapted. The actual method, the Ghost Walk, the Cat Walk, and the Kitten Crawl, varies according to the distance you are from your quarry and the type of country you are moving through, but all the time you must use cunning and move stealthily.

The ghost walk

To walk quietly in the dark demands greater use of touch. Feel the ground in front with the toe before placing the foot fully down. Hold the hands in front of you and slowly move them up and down the full length of the body to detect branches, wires or

Figure 20   The ghost walk

the person in front of you if you are part of a team. An alternative to using the hand is to use a thin stick in one hand and to move this up and down.

The cat walk
The technique for this is to crawl on your hands and knees, search the ground ahead for noise-making vegetation. You move the knee forwards to where your hand has searched.

Figure 21   The cat walk

The kitten crawl
This is quiet but slow. It is also very tiring. The stalker has to lie on his front. He searches ahead for noise-making vegetation. Then he lifts his body on his forearms and toes. He presses forward and then lowers his body gently to the ground.

Figure 22   The kitten crawl

In summary:
- At night remember you hear and smell more than you see – turn your ears towards any sound
- Stop and listen, keep close to the ground
- Freeze if you hear a noise
- Keep quiet
- Don't have loose equipment
- Move carefully. Use the ghost walk, the cat walk, or the kitten crawl
- Clear your route
- Don't step on dry vegetation
- Use any available cover
- Be aware that vehicle lights turn night into day
- Use your ears
- If the quarry is near check on his movements frequently by putting an ear close to the ground
- Breathing into the air on cold nights will create an obvious cloud above the stalker – breathe into your jacket or the grass or disperse your breath with a scarf

A NOTE ON SAFETY FOR INSTRUCTORS

There are so many valuable lessons to be learnt out of a night stalk that it is an essential part of any stalking training and therefore any tracking training.

But any person involved with training, especially training young people, must take note of a safety point. It is foolish, almost criminal, to initiate night stalking training on an individual basis – this must be built up to.

We all have a fear of the dark. The trees and fences become magnified, sounds become intensified, the ground becomes more uneven, until gradually we feel a sinking sensation inside which warns us that it is time to take a grip of ourselves. When we have become accustomed to these apparent changes we begin to appreciate the subtle beauty of the dark and become quick to read the noises of the night.

Walk out at night, in a group at first, and practise by listening for sounds and learning their meaning, by looking at the stars and the lighter horizon, by distinguishing shadows from objects at a distance, by using the sense of smell to find out what is happening round about, and by feeling and identifying different objects in the dark. Become accustomed to the unfamiliar by degrees. Then stalks should be arranged for pairs before individual night stalks are attempted.

CHAPTER TWELVE

The Track Pursuit Drill

We now have the theoretical knowledge, and if the earlier exercises have been mastered in the field, also the practical experience to study meaningfully the linchpin of tracking – the track pursuit drill.

The track pursuit drill (TPD) is a distillation of lessons learnt in the art of tracking. It has been devised and formulated by the military so as to provide a framework from which the tracker can work. It is particularly useful for the student because he has the guidance of a sequence. So, as its name suggests, the TPD is a sequence of activities, a drill, which the tracker employs whilst in the pursuit of his quarry. Some of the steps in the sequence are thought processes and some are actions. If the drill is followed in its correct sequence it gives the tracker the best chance of following his quarry. There are seven steps which are, in effect, a cycle and when the end of the cycle is reached the sequence is started again – this drill continues until the culmination of the track.

This chapter introduces the process of interpretation of sign and its interrelationship with the TPD. It gives an overview of the TPD's seven steps leading into a full explanation of each stage of the process.

INTERPRETATION OF SIGN

Once a person knows what to look for following the sign can be likened to following a series of sign posts. But for the sign to become obvious the tracker must first interpret what he has observed.

The following assists the student in interpreting the sign:
- The sign must be studied very carefully
- Distinguish the sign from among the many others
- As soon as possible, the condition of the quarry being

followed must be assessed, that is, whether it is lazy, tired, alert, confident, or any other indication as to its state

- Idiosyncracies and traits must be noted
- Any slight change, no matter how small it is, in its sign must be investigated thoroughly
- Anticipate the quarry's moves, the direction of travel, and any likely deceptions
- Build up a complete picture from all the available sign
- Continuously monitor the ground and country in relation to the direction of travel

AN OVERVIEW OF THE TRACK PURSUIT DRILL

For the visual tracker to be able to follow and make contact with the quarry the TPD must be implemented. There are seven separate steps to this drill. Each step has been formulated for a specific purpose and it is essential that every potential tracker learns and at all times follows this drill. I will now give you a brief outline of the drill and then analyse each stage separately.

Step 1: assessment of the general direction
The tracker looks ahead along the perceived track to the maximum visibility and back to where he is standing for the general direction of the track.

Step 2: eliminate all openings and finalise the general direction
If there are two or more openings, compare the ages and eliminate old tracks – assuming you know the track that you are following is the most recent one.

Step 3: look for the furthest sign and connect it back to your position
This is to ensure that there is not a split track or that no other form of deception has been practised. This ensures that you, the visual tracker, are still following the same track.

Step 4: look through the vegetation for the quarry
This step is, in reality, an ongoing process and that is the reason it is placed mid-way through the sequence. It is very important and must be carried out at every opportunity. The visual tracker

must always be aware of the possibility that the quarry is close.

Step 5: check the area to the left and right for deception tactics

By carrying out this drill you ensure that your quarry has not gone off your line of travel and that there isn't any access to the sides. There are many ways in which the quarry can confuse the tracker and these will be dealt with in full in Chapter Thirteen. This step is to combat being led astray.

Step 6: plan and memorise your next footsteps

Here the tracker is working out the best route to the furthest sign which was made by the quarry. The tracker makes a mental note of all obstacles which will have to be negotiated because once he starts to move forward he will be looking ahead and not at the ground. He memorises the footsteps and notes particularly any sound-making vegetation. It is important to remember that in steps 1 to 6 the tracker has remained for the most part stationary. This is because the eyes do most of the work. You are alert to all sounds, smells, movement and vegetation in an unnatural state. Remember we are minimising all unnecessary movement which could give our position away.

Step 7: move forward with stealth

The most vulnerable time for the visual tracker is when he is moving. Any sudden movement might catch the quarry's eye. This will result in the quarry being put to flight or, in the case of a military tracker, in your being ambushed. The tracker must retain a mental picture of the track and the footsteps to be taken. With the head held up and the eyes carrying out the drills the tracker moves forward, alert to all areas ahead and for any sign of the quarry. Trackers must develop good peripheral vision. When the tracker arrives at the furthest sign of the quarry he again visually checks all the area to the front for the quarry's presence before restarting the cycle.

For ease of explanation the following description is based on an area with vegetation but, although tracking in desert areas or anywhere without vegetation may be harder, the same basic principals of the TPD can still be applied. Let us now have a more detailed look at the seven steps of the TPD.

STEP 1: ASSESSMENT OF THE GENERAL DIRECTION (Figure 23)
Start tracking from a definite point where the signs are those made by the intended quarry, for example, outside an earth, a sett, a den, a burrow, a nest, a camp site, or an incident area. If this is not possible, you are going to have to rely on information about a sighting of the quarry itself from a reliable source. For the nature conservationist this may be a fellow club member, for the military tracker this may be from the local security forces. Once in the immediate area of the sighting your first task is to stand back and observe the area as a whole for the quarry itself. Use binoculars for this in open country. On drawing a blank you must then close in on the location of the last sighting of the quarry and cast about the immediate area until you locate the quarry's track, sign, or spoor.

Once a start point has been confirmed, look carefully at all signs in the immediate area and estimate the age of the sign. This can be checked against the information received from your informant. If your sign is two to three days old and the sighting of the quarry took place four hours ago you are on the wrong track. The physical evidence and your information should confirm each other. If not you must, repeat the casting drill (see Chapter Sixteen) again until you locate and verify the correct sign left by your quarry.

At the start of the track try and estimate the number in the party or group, or the numbers and types of vehicles. By estimating the age of the sign and the number of quarry at the start of the track you will subsequently be in a better position to recognise the following:

- Where the quarry has rested
- Overnight stopping sites
- Watering points
- Feeding areas

It is highly probable that you will find fresh tracks over old tracks at many of the places mentioned above and that the quarry may have moved off again in a different direction. The track that you are following may well have foul tracks on top of it, giving you the problem of distinguishing old from new and verifying which is your track.

Now stand beside the last definite sign facing in the general direction the quarry was last travelling in and look ahead twenty to thirty metres. Look for all the possible openings made in the undergrowth and trees to determine the general direction of the track. These openings are recognised and become apparent by eliminating areas where the quarry could not possibly have moved through, such as natural obstacles, and where there has been no breaking of the undergrowth or disturbance to the vegetation – no physical sign. It is possible that two or three openings or the undergrowth to your front are large enough for the quarry to have passed through. Ensure that you have checked the complete area to your front and also that you are looking as far ahead as is possible and through the undergrowth for any possible signs or sightings of the quarry.

Put yourself in the quarry's place and ask yourself, 'Which way would I go?' If the quarry is unaware that it is being followed, you can often locate the general direction of travel quite easily. Step 1 of the TPD has established the general direction of travel.

STEP 2: ELIMINATE ALL OPENINGS AND FINALISE THE GENERAL DIRECTION (Figure 24)

Whenever an animal or human moves through any environment they will always cause disturbance that in some way will alter the natural appearance along the 'line of march' when compared with the surroundings. A tracker, through training and experience, begins to recognise these changes and by a process of elimination is able to narrow the options down to the most probable direction of the 'line of march'.

Take each opening in turn and carry out the following drill:
- Look forward to the maximum visibility for ground and top sign
- Remember the age of the track that you are following and do not be drawn forward by ground and top sign which is of a different age to your track
- Eliminate openings to the left and right which do not coincide with the age of your quarry's track
- Endeavour to end up with one opening which you now perceive to be the general direction of the track left by the quarry. If it is not possible to eliminate all the openings except one and you end up with two options then you must:

      – Remember the possibility of a split track, that is, when a group separates and takes different routes

      – Remember, if there is a definite split, you should follow the quarry which has left the most sign

      – Remember that you may have two or more general directions but on inspection all but one can be eliminated

Having completed Step 2 of the TPD you should have eliminated the openings and finalised the 'general direction'.

STEP 3: LOOK FOR THE FURTHEST SIGN AND CONNECT IT BACK TO YOUR POSITION (Figure 25)

If it has been established that there are visual tracking signs to your front of the right age and that the quarry could have physically passed from where you are standing to the point where you have sighted the furthest sign, we are then ready for Step 3 of the TPD which is to confirm that the track which we have followed so far is, in fact, the same track as that spotted out front. Without moving from your position you then look at the furthest sign, backtrack with your eyes, noting signs along the way to link up the furthermost sign with your present position. Here the tracker is going through a process to confirm that the track being followed is the clearest track. This backtracking with the eyes and connecting up signs will often serve to eliminate false openings and false tracks.

A visual tracker must not get into the habit of connecting up track from the nearest sign to the next sign ahead unless he is specifically carrying out pace tracking (see Chapters Two and Seventeen). The reason for this is twofold. Firstly, it is quicker – if you have good top sign and conclusive ground sign twenty to thirty metres to your front you can move straight on. The tracker has to be conscious of the fact that as the distance increases between him and the quarry the track gets older, colder and more difficult to follow. Secondly, if an inexperienced tracker is concentrating on the ground sign and pace tracking (a procedure which is sometimes unavoidable but very time consuming) he is likely to miss an actual sighting of the quarry ahead.

It is important to mention here that a tracker should always

Figures 23, 24 & 25   The track pursuit drill

have conclusive or substantiating sign in front before proceeding to the next stage, especially in areas where little sign is left due to the nature of the terrain. During the early learning stage it is advisable that the visual tracker stands just behind the last definite sign and not on it whilst carrying out the TPD, so as not to obliterate the sign by your own. This is just in case you need to refer to the last definite sign again, as in the lost track drills (see Chapter Sixteen).

To examine ground sign immediately in front of him the tracker goes down slowly onto one knee. He doesn't attempt to examine it from a standing position because his forward peripheral vision is severely reduced and also he needs to get as close to the sign as possible to observe all the detail.

The method of looking ahead and then connecting the furthest sign back to the tracker's position has many advantages:

- Speed – as mentioned above
- Split tracks are easier to identify
- The track picture becomes more obvious with the tracker merely using individual signs to confirm the track picture

STEP 4: LOOK THROUGH THE VEGETATION FOR THE QUARRY

At this stage the tracker has not yet moved forward but we know that the track has been established and confirmed for the next twenty to thirty metres. Depending on the type of quarry, you will be looking at ground level, in the trees, in the sky, or even underground.

In Step 4 the visual tracker must visually clear the area to the front. This should also be done before the commencement of Step 1, that is, at the end of Step 7, as the TPD is a cycle. This is a continuous process but it is included here as a separate step halfway through the TPD because:

- During the intervening period the quarry may have moved into the area
- To emphasise the importance of attuning oneself to being aware of the quarry's presence and the possible danger associated with it

If necessary, the tracker crouches or kneels to check at ground level through the vegetation. He checks through the tunnel-type runs which are made by the constant use of animals. The tracker should move from side to side so that areas behind obstacles can be seen.

We have now proved the track out to twenty or thirty metres. We have built up the track picture and feel confident that the quarry is not in the immediate area.

Remember look through the vegetation not at it!

STEP 5: CHECK THE AREAS TO THE LEFT AND RIGHT FOR DECEPTION TACTICS

Deception tactics are mainly the concern of trackers working with the military or the law enforcement agencies. Both the enemy soldier and the criminal can be expected to use various forms of deception tactics to hinder or even ambush the tracker and his team. There are many ways of confusing a tracker or follow-up party. These tactics will be covered in detail in Chapter Thirteen.

We are now in the position where the track has been established and confirmed and we have checked out the immediate area and have not sighted the quarry. The police or military tracker has to be as sure as is possible that the fugitive or enemy are not present, that they are not in ambush positions, or that they have not laid booby traps. It is vitally important that the military tracker has a full understanding of the types of booby traps associated with the enemy that he is tracking.

Step 5 is not solely for trackers following a human quarry. Some of the large game animals have been known to ambush the unwary hunter by circling around behind him.

The visual tracker must now concentrate on detecting any deception tactics which the quarry have used to lead the visual tracker astray. The tracker looks along the confirmed track, concentrating on the areas to the left and right of the track to check for signs of 'drop-off' tracks. The slightest irregularity to the vegetation will be noted for confirmation later during Step 7. The tracker must have a thorough knowledge and understanding of all known deception tactics and must always be conscious of their possible use.

On occasions a visual tracker may deliberately follow up on a deception tactic to gain a greater understanding of the quarry. The cunning and cleverness, the degree of alertness and stealth with which a deception tactic has been carried out will certainly assist the visual tracker in understanding the way the quarry thinks and acts. Getting to know and understand the reasoning, thinking process and habits of the quarry will assist the visual tracker in making an intelligent appreciation of the quarry's intentions. If ever the track is completely lost, the tracker will be in a better position to make an appreciation and assumptions of where to look when carrying out the 'Likely Areas Probe' which will be covered in detail in Chapter Sixteen.

STEP 6: PLAN AND MEMORISE YOUR NEXT FOOTSTEPS
(Figure 26)

The track has been located, confirmed, there have been no sightings of the quarry and the areas left and right of the track have been scrutinised for deception tactics.

In Step 6 the tracker has to work out the best route to the furthest sign, making a mental note of all obstacles which will have to be negotiated. The principle behind this is that the tracker should only move forward whilst observing the area to his front – not the ground and where he is going to place his feet.

The tracker now looks at the ground. He notes and memorises the placement of each foot for the move forward to the farthest sign or the next ten to twenty steps. The tracker will note roots and vines across the track which could possibly catch the feet. I have seen many trainee trackers take a tumble when moving forward because they have not studied the ground in sufficient detail.

Noise is another factor for consideration at this juncture. The tracker will not wish to place a foot on or through any vegetation which would create a noise. In areas of dense vegetation noise will often travel farther than one can see, so particular care is required so as not to alert the quarry to your presence.

Bearing in mind that nature will not move vegetation in isolation, the visual tracker should note all vegetation to the front which, if disturbed, could cause the movement of isolated branches, tree tops, bushes, or any other interconnected vegetation. These can telegraph the tracker's presence ahead. When moving through areas of close vegetation the inexperienced or tired person will often be heard first and then give their position away by movement of the undergrowth before they are actually sighted. At this stage the visual tracker has not taken one step forward. During Step 4 the tracker has merely moved from side to side and up and down. In Steps 1 to 6 for the most part the tracker has remained stationary with his head up and looking ahead so that he can immediately catch any movement and hear the slightest sound to his front.

Remember we are minimising all unnecessary movement which could compromise the tracker's position.

STEP 7: MOVE FORWARD WITH STEALTH (Figure 27)

The tracker now moves forward with stealth to the limit of the confirmed track. He places each foot on the predetermined locations. It is important to note that, at this stage, new areas to the front will be opening up – areas which have not been thoroughly checked. Once moving, the tracker becomes more vulnerable and obvious to any watching quarry.

The visual tracker when moving forward must never look at the ground. He has no need to after the study he made of it in Step 6. If the tracker does need to check the ground or confirm possible deception tactics he must stop, go down on one knee and inspect the ground. To endorse the significance of this point in the military context the tracker always has a 'cover man' following at a suitable distance behind in order to protect the tracker.

Whilst moving forward, the tracker ensures that his position is not telegraphed ahead by undue movement of vegetation. He must also ensure that no sounds are made which could travel beyond limits covered by his vision. During this step the tracker is trying to spot, locate, and discover the quarry without the quarry being alerted to his or his team's presence.

If no quarry is sighted, and this will happen most of the time when the visual tracker arrives at the furthermost point and before beginning Step 1 again, the tracker will visually check all the area to the front for signs of the quarry. The drill is repeated over and over until the information about the quarry is obtained or contact is made.

AN EXAMPLE OF THE TPD IN ACTION

The scene is set in a cold temperate area, in spring. The start point of the follow was a sighting in the early hours of the morning by a dairy farmer. He saw a small group of soldiers crossing the road by his farm. They seemed to be carrying one of their colleagues on a stretcher. We've been following the patrol of soldiers for three kilometres through mixed farmland. It has been easy to deduce that the group is eight men strong by a close study of their prints as they passed along a clay section of

Figures 26 & 27   The track pursuit drill

ground (see Chapter Fifteen for details). Also we have confirmed that they are carrying a heavy stretcher by the impression it makes in the ground when they change over bearers. The last section across a dew-soaked field was very clear before the sun evaporated the moisture. We have now entered deciduous woodland. The ground sign is a great deal less obvious. It is now a question of applying the TPD more slowly than before. We approach the entry point into the wood very cautiously, as this would be an ideal place to ambush any pursuers, but as they have a casualty and their border is near they are probably going as fast as they can for safety.

Step 1: assessment of the general direction. I look through the trees. They are widely spaced mature oaks with little undergrowth, but my first thought is to ensure the area is clear of the quarry – it is. The continuation of the direction across the field into the wood is blocked by a small rocky outcrop which angles away to the left. The direction could either be angling away along the outcrop or they have turned sharp right and paralleled the treeline.

Step 2: eliminate all openings and finalise the general direction. To the right the dead vegetation on the forest floor is undisturbed.

Along the line of the rocks there is an indication of leaves being disturbed. To the left of this the ground is pristine.

Step 3: look for the furthest sign and connect it back to your position. Five metres along this line is a riverlet. On the far bank are numerous skid marks. This is the stretcher party negotiating the obstacle.

Step 4: look through the vegetation for the quarry. The rocky outcrop to my right is cause for concern but after a prolonged scrutiny nothing untoward is registered.

Step 5: check the area to the left and right for deception tactics. Nothing is evident.

Step 6: plan and memorise your footsteps. The first couple of paces are on mossy ground – no trouble there with noise. But just before the stream there's an area covered with old dry twigs. I identify a couple of places where I can place my feet without cracking the twigs.

Step 7: move forward with stealth. Keeping looking to the front, scanning and searching the vegetation for the quarry, I proceed to the next sign, which turns out to be conclusive as we can identify several of the individual boot prints in the mud on the stream bank.

This will give you an indication of the type of thoughts that are going through the tracker's mind as he continually runs through the TPD.

OVERSHOOTING A TRACK

There is a specific drill laid down for the eventuality that the tracker loses the track – it will be dealt with fully in Chapter Sixteen, but the student should note at this stage the indications that he has overshot the track. They are:

- Individual tracking signs, conclusive or substantiating, are absent
- The ground is fresh – each step will cause leaves and small twigs to crack and break, worm casts will crush and the general under-foot feel will be different
- Cobwebs that would normally be broken by the quarry you are following are intact, especially in the morning
- Dew is still present on the vegetation and ground, whereas it should have been brushed aside by the quarry if the sun has not had a chance to evaporate the moisture

- Vegetation as a whole will be in a natural state, showing no signs of disturbance, colour change, or pointers and you, the tracker, will find yourself making new openings in the undergrowth

The tracker's first problem now is not finding the track but exercising self-control. Sit down and silently deliberate about the chances of re-establishing the track. Take plenty of time to think. Then look carefully and patiently.

Never give up
The trail is there
Somewhere!

THE FUTURE AND SOME ENCOURAGEMENT

The full Track Pursuit Drill may seem a laborious process but during the early periods potential trackers must follow each step of the TPD until the sequence becomes second nature. Eventually, as competence and confidence improve, the visual tracker will be able to combine steps, performing several parts of the procedure with one quick glance and the periods of time spent between successive steps will soon become imperceptibly short pauses.

Another seemingly insurmountable obstacle will be stealthy movement but this also will become as natural as taking a breath.

In conclusion, remember the seven steps:

1 Assessment of the general direction
2 Eliminate all openings and finalise the general direction
3 Look for the furthest sign and connect it back to your position
4 Look through the vegetation for the quarry
5 Check the area to the left and right for deception tactics
6 Plan and memorise your next footsteps
7 Move forward with stealth

CHAPTER THIRTEEN

Deception Tactics

This chapter is primarily applicable to tracking a human quarry.

It is a physical fact that a human will always leave sign of his presence. The conspicuousness of the sign depends on the environmental factors which we discussed in Chapter Four but the value of the sign is dependent upon the experience of the tracker.

Any military unit or any fugitives who consider that their pursuers will deploy trackers will be very wise to employ deception plans. The aim of any deception is to gain time and distance and in some military contexts to ambush the pursuers.

A look at basic deception tactics will make the tracker realise that there are many different ways in which a determined quarry can confuse, delay and possibly lose a tracker and his team. Determination and imagination will often need to be called on by the tracker when tracking through deception tactics. But unless the group laying the deception plan is extremely efficient, they will more often than not signpost their deception by leaving a piece of sign which is obviously out of place to the experienced eye of the tracker.

The following is a list of the deception methods that can be employed:

- Walking backwards
- Conversion of sign
- Brushing the track
- Stone hopping
- Tip toe walking
- Fade out
- Splitting up if the quarry is in a group
- Crossing or walking in a stream or river bed
- Looping back

A sophisticated enemy may deploy a whole series of deception methods to make the tracker team waste time and effort. But even this, although it slows the tracker, is in itself an indication as to the state of the enemy – they are alert, highly skilled and therefore very dangerous. The military tracker would then be seriously considering the possibility of the track being booby trapped or of his team being ambushed.

I will now detail each of the major deception methods. With each tactic I will indicate the clues which tell a tracker that a deception tactic is being employed against him. The student will notice that some of the methods are more appropriate to certain types of environment than others.

WALKING BACKWARDS

This is the equivalent of Dick Turpin putting the horse shoes back to front on Black Bess – it would throw the unobservant tracker off the line of march by a complete 180 degrees. But to the tracker aware of this ploy it is as clear as day for several reasons:

- When a person walks backwards the length of his pace is shortened
- The toe and the ball of the foot will be more pronounced, the heel not so much
- Loose dirt, dust, sand, long grass, ferns, and foliage will still be dragged in the direction of movement (see Chapter Two – Pointers)
- The feet are placed wider apart for balance

CONVERSION OF SIGN

Unless a person is reasonably good, this practice only serves to sign post his direction. People sometimes try to mask their prints by making animal tracks over them, usually pig tracks, by the use of shaped sticks.

BRUSHING OVER THE TRACKS

Again to an experienced tracker this technique only signposts the track and thus the intentions. The quarry attempts to hide his sign by brushing over it or placing over it leaves, sticks, stones, and earth. The sign leads to the area that has been brushed, the tracker has then to ask himself why did they brush the track at this point and where did they go.

STONE HOPPING

This is attempted as a deception if there is an area of large stones that are firm and do not move when stepped on. The stones or rocks have to be very large otherwise there will be sign left, because after a stone has lain for some time, dirt and sand will build up around the base. Once stepped on, this wall will crumble and what appears to be a shadow will appear around the base – a colouration difference at the lower edge of the stone. This is an extremely difficult and arduous deception tactic to follow especially if it is used for some distance.

One strong indication is that there will be fine particles of dust, sand or dirt left on the surface of the stone – transfer of sign.

TIP TOE WALKING

This is a very tiring procedure and is well nigh impossible over a long distance. It is relatively easy for a good tracker to detect because the toe is obviously very prominent and the pace is much shorter.

FADE OUT

This is where members of the group jump off the track. The tracker should notice the amount of sign being tracked and that it is starting to dwindle. By checking the sides of the track you should be able to find the 'jump off' points. These can give a surprising amount of intelligence about a group as it becomes more relaxed, assuming that the deception has worked. A fade out may be the enemy's start to his daily lying-up drills or even his preparations for an ambush on your party. This sophisticated, co-ordinated technique should alert the tracker.

SPLITTING UP

This is similar to the fade out. In fact at first it is indistinguishable from the fade out but with the latter the tracker will start noticing that the group has started to reunite. Again the indication to the tracker is that the amount of sign decreases. The rule in this case is to follow the sign which is the most prominent or where the sign indicates the larger group went.

CROSSING OR WALKING IN A STREAM BED

It is normally done where the water is rippling in the vain hope that it makes the sign much harder to locate, whereas in fact it makes it easier because the small stones on the stream bed are disturbed and their light undersides revealed. If the quarry cross in deep water exit points will normally be prominent as water splashes will be transferred, muddy banks marked and over-hanging branches used to pull themselves out.

LOOPING

Although not strictly speaking a tracking deception tactic, I feel that it is worth mentioning here to give a full picture of what is mainly military tracking. If the track starts to change direction in a gradual but similar direction, thus describing a loop, it is a fair assumption that the enemy have looped their track so that any follow-up party will be passing in front of their observation position. Depending on the freshness of the track this could be dangerous but if the sign is old, a tracker should be thinking about seizing the opportunity of coming across an old lying-up position to gain intelligence about the enemy.

In conclusion, it is extremely important for a tracker to have an understanding of deception tactics and any person involved with the training of trackers should build into the training the use of deception tactics during the middle stages of the course in a gradual and controlled fashion.

If trackers can identify deception tactics used by the quarry they will be able to counter them and it will give them a greater understanding of the quarry.

Always remember deception tactics are mainly used by man and that man, when he is a quarry, is a very dangerous animal. He uses deception tactics against trackers for three main reasons:

To gain time
To lose the tracking team
TO KILL THE TRACKER

CHAPTER FOURTEEN

Judging the Age of Sign

The student of tracking who has been applying the skills so far described in this book will now be realising how important it is to be able to give an accurate estimate of the age of the sign. The last chapter highlights this fact in what may be a life or death situation.

The present chapter and the next will enhance the practical skills of the tracker. We are now moving more and more into the area of the application of our reasoning powers.

Judging the age of a track is the most difficult aspect of visual tracking and can only be achieved with confidence and a good degree of accuracy after practice and experience in an environment.

THE IMPORTANCE OF THE TIME BRACKET
The sign needs to be placed into a time bracket for the following reasons:
- To distinguish between old and fresh sign
- To determine the approximate time lapse since the quarry passed through the area – this will give you some indication of your position in relation to that of your quarry
- To establish the correct track picture – this is building up the story of the trail as a whole and it is imperative that the time bracket is assessed correctly in order that no confusion occurs in the tracker's mind
- To use foul tracks to your advantage and not to be misled by them
- To gather information for use by intelligence analysts

THE FOUR FACTORS
It was stated in Chapter Four that four factors affect the quarry's sign, that is:
- Time

- Features of the terrain
- Climatic conditions
- Spoor and sign left by third parties

We are now going to separate out the time element and study how sign alters over time with the others factors remaining constant.

THE TERRAIN AS A MEDIUM

It is worthwhile in many cases to view the physical terrain as a medium upon which the quarry writes or draws as he passes over or through it. What he writes is the sign. What we are now interested in is whether the medium has a nature which will retain the sign or not, and if so, for how long.

The concept of permanency of the sign was hinted at in Chapter Three when two of the classifications of sign were given as permanent or temporary. It is useful to consider the physical surface for the purposes of judging the age of the sign as being:

- Soft – where disturbance or damage is easily inflicted, for example: soft soil, mud, sand, snow, green leafy plants, ferns, crops, grasses, roots that bleed, most types of dead or dry foliage (leaves, pine needles), ant hills, worm casts, and animal droppings.
- Hard – being matter or material that is resistant to damage or disturbance, for example: hard packed or sun-baked soil, frozen ground, rocky ground, roads, tracks, resilient mosses, tussock grass, many man-made objects (plastic, metal – usually classed as discardables in tracking terms).

EXPOSURE TO THE CLIMATE – WEATHERING

As we have isolated the time part of the formula we have now to concern ourselves with not only the climatic factors but how long they exert their influence on the sign. If the medium upon which the sign is written is exposed to the elements it will obviously be affected more than sign which is sheltered from the weather.

An example will illustrate the point. An object such as a piece of cloth, a newspaper, a used fire, animal droppings will age at a different rate depending upon whether they are in a ploughed field or under the canopy of a thick forest.

The tracker has to assess the exposure of the sign and has then to remember the weather over the preceding period.

To be able to judge age accurately to within hours will only come with experience and continual application and practice. And however talented the tracker is, certain types of environment will only give him a broad time bracket in which to place the quarry's passage. But, with the skills of the next chapter, the most difficult terrain may reveal the quarry's secrets to within a few minutes, if all the evidence is used.

Having considered the type of physical surface (the medium), and how much or how little it has been exposed to the climatic elements, the tracker has now to use other techniques to attain a greater degree of accuracy. The following are the methods available to assist his judgement.

COMPARISON OF COLOUR
An indication of the age of a track may be gained by the state of dryness of cracks and splits that appear in grasses that have been trodden on or disturbed. When fresh they are green, but after a few days they turn a brown colour.

BREAKING AND COMPARING STICKS AND TWIGS
A tracker who is trying to use a break in a twig, for instance, to assess the time when the quarry passed by may break a similar piece of vegetation and compare the fresh break with that which the quarry made. A fresh break will be a lighter colour and a study of the ends may show fibres protruding. These fibres disappear over a period of time and the colour darkens.

COMPARISON OF IMPRESSION
By comparing your print beside that of the quarry's and contrasting the colour change and the degree of definition an assessment can be made of the age of the quarry's sign.

TIME BRACKETS CREATED BY PRECIPITATION
Rain, mist or dew will pock mark tracks and they will appear to lack definition. Therefore these sorts of tracks will have been made before or during the rain. If they are not pock marked they will have been made after the rain. This pock marking can be

Figure 28 Comparing a freshly broken twig with the sign

caused by mist or dew dripping from trees which, when considered by a tracker with knowledge of the local weather conditions, will give an estimate of the age. An example will explain: if a track was found at midday and there was a heavy downfall of rain at 0200 hours, and the track was clear, you can say it was made since the rain, placing it into a ten-hour time bracket.

WIND

In forests, leaves and pine needles are always falling from trees. The amount of foliage that falls on the sign will depend on the season and on the wind and precipitation over the period since the quarry passed – this is a further indication of the age of the tracks.

SUPERIMPOSED GAME TRACKS

Most wild animals lie up during the day and move at night and many species such as deer will move up and down the same track to and from their resting place to their source of food and water. If human prints on a main game trail have animal tracks superimposed and these tracks show that the animal has moved in both directions the tracker can estimate that the human prints are probably at least one night old. If the tracks show that the animal has moved only in one direction, then human tracks were probably made during the night – after the animal has moved down to water and before it has moved back.

WILDLIFE

By studying and noting the habits of the wildlife with regards to feeding, watering, and movement, the tracker can gain information which will assist him in assessing the age of the quarry's sign. As mentioned, most wild animals feed and move during the hours of darkness but most birds feed during the day and if they lay sign which affects or is affected by the quarry's sign, knowledge of the timings of their activities gives the tracker another time bracket with which to encapsulate the quarry.

Apart from disturbances to worm casts and insect life, as noted below, the existence of broken cobwebs should also be taken into consideration to try and place your quarry's movement within a period. Awareness of all your natural surroundings will be a great aid in judging the age of sign.

PRINTS IN MUD

The state of dryness of a track in mud or soft ground must be noted. If the track is very fresh, water will not have run back into the depression made by the quarry's footprint. Later the water runs back, and later still the mud which has been pushed up around the print and kicked forward by the quarry's foot leaving the ground begins to dry.

EXPOSED EARTH

Freshly exposed earth, whether dug or ploughed, has a unique smell and a characteristic appearance. Weather and exposure will eventually take away the fresh smell and the new look. Closer examination of freshly disturbed earth will reveal two things. Firstly, it smells different because the newly exposed earth uncovers a greater area of freshly disturbed, squashed, crushed roots and insects, but more importantly it contains more moisture. It is this when it begins to evaporate that gives off the distinctive odours. Secondly, it will be noted that freshly disturbed earth is in a completely unnatural position – clods and lumps of earth will be balanced one upon the other. This is the state of freshly disturbed earth whether it is ploughed, dug or, of more interest to the tracker, disturbed by the passage of the quarry.

The visual tracker will see the similarities between the fresh skid, slide and scuff marks of the quarry and the newly dug or ploughed piece of earth. Shoes, hooves and pads leave exposed earth. When this is fresh it will have flat surfaces with straight edges outlining the pattern of the print. Both the colour and the

Figure 29 How water refills a print

smell will be different, close examination will show many examples of small particles – grains of sand, soil, and mud balancing one upon the other. As the sign becomes exposed to the elements the wind, rain, sun and snow will start to blow away the finely powdered earth and level the balancing grains. The heat of the sun will dry up and age the whole appearance and alter the smell radically. The fresh print has now changed its appearance, it has become dull in colour, vague and unclear.

If the ground is frozen or very sandy it will react more like rock or pure sand respectively.

DRY LEAVES

With a fresh track over dry leaves the visual tracker will have to look for the following. The overall disturbances will cause a different colour and appearance to the surrounding area. The effect will be greater shadow and so a darker colour. Tilted leaves will be in an unbalanced state. Each leaf that has been stepped on will either bend, break or crumble and the edges of broken and torn leaves will be lighter in colour to those of weathered surfaces. On freshly walked over leaves there will be more evidence of transfer (see Chapter Two). Rain will pat each leaf down into its natural position and so eliminate shadow and colour, sand on leaves and the smaller particles of leaves will be washed off. As the sign is exposed to weathering the transferred material will tend to be removed. Unbalanced leaves will resettle themselves. The darker shadowing will disappear as the old pattern re-establishes itself. If sunshine follows rain after twenty-four hours all signs of freshness will have gone from this sort of sign. The exposed, freshly broken ends will begin to darken and the fibrous ends will curl up and disappear.

STICKS

What has been said above about leaves applies equally to sticks and twigs, with the addition that often the undersides will be darker in colour and may possibly have small particles of either sand or decaying vegetation adhering to them.

GROWING VEGETATION

The state and position of trodden vegetation must be noted. Various grasses have different degrees of resilience and prior knowledge of the response of flora to being crushed, pushed aside, broken, cut and squashed will assist in determining the age of the sign.

Only by studying flora present in areas of operation over a period of time can the tracker become skilful with this method.

Think of a vase of freshly picked flowers with no water and put out in direct sunlight – they will soon wither and die. In water and in shade they will stay fresh and alive-looking for a much longer time. Next think of the many different kinds of flowers, some of which when cut and given water and shade will last only two to three days, while others will be in bloom over two weeks later. The visual tracker should be aware of these differences in ageing.

Pulpy leaves with a high water content will wither and die faster than vegetation with a low water content. The tip leaves of most branches which are the new tender leaves, will be the first to show signs of ageing. Plants with a low water content when subjected to heavy rain will rot and darken in colour at a rapid rate.

The visual tracker must also be aware of a plant's reactions to cutting, breaking, or bruising.

So far I have described the effect on the removed section – the growing section must also be considered. First, sap will appear then congeal or dry up. Next when the cut end has dried it will start to turn brown. The speed of browning will differ with different species and exposure to weathering.

Growth will begin again from the next bud or shoot down. The process can take from two to nine months, depending on the species.

MAN-MADE OBJECTS

If man is the quarry he will probably have many man-made items with him for his support. These can be broadly categorised into items for sustenance, medical, sleeping and shelter, navigation, weapons, and communications. When a visual tracker locates an old camping site or a recently vacated one, he will need to know the speed of ageing of the different items listed to estimate when the camp was last used. You will need to know that, for instance, a metal can which is constructed to hold a liquid with acid content will be more durable and stay newer-looking longer than metal constructed to hold a liquid with an alkali base. The quality of the product, which can be determined to some extent by the country of manufacture, should also be noted, as this affects the speed of ageing. The tracker should be able to assess the age of a variety of objects such as: paper products, including cigarette packets, writing paper, sweet papers, newspaper, as well as textiles, plastics and metal objects.

FIRES

Fires can be an invaluable guide to a tracker if the particular fire site can be linked to the quarry. Not only does the retained heat at various levels give an indication of the fire's recent use – up to twenty-four hours ago – but the changes to the ash brought about by rainfall and to the food remains by decomposition can give clues which indicate the age of the sign.

WORM CASTS

In the early hours of the morning these are soft, after they have been exposed to the sun for some time they dry out. Therefore, armed with this knowledge and his memory of the exposure that the cast will have had to sunlight (local weather conditions), the tracker can estimate the time bracket. The quarry will have either trodden on the ground before the worm appeared and therefore the cast will be superimposed on his print, or the quarry will have trodden on a moist cast which will produce a flat circular formation, or a dry one, in which case the cast will be powdery.

ANTS AND TERMITES

Ants and termites on the move can give you a good indication of the time the quarry passed by, as long as you know by conclusive sign that it was your quarry that disturbed them. Depending on the amount of damage inflicted on them by the quarry, it can take them up to two hours to resume their natural formations.

ANIMAL DROPPINGS

All animals produce either solid or semi-solid faeces. Although there can be a variation within a species and even from the same animal depending upon its age, condition, and its diet, usually droppings can be used to identify a species. But more usefully, the state of the droppings can be used as a time indicator. This can either be used if tracking the animal who produced the droppings or the droppings can be the medium for the quarry's sign.

The fact that many animals are creatures of habit and have regular defecating places and use their urine and scent glands to mark their areas can also assist the tracker in placing either the animal's movements or some other quarry's movements within a time bracket if the tracker is familiar with his environment.

SMELL

Smell, whether the sap from a freshly cut branch, wood smoke hanging in still air, or the smell of freshly dug animal homes, recent droppings, or newly marked scent posts will all indicate a fresh track. Where there is no smell this will indicate that the sign is not fresh.

AN ADVANCED TECHNIQUE – AGE STANDS

If a professional tracker is intending to operate in an area over a protracted period, or if he is training other trackers to operate in an area (see Chapter Seventeen), he will employ the following method to enhance his skills in judging the age of sign and provide continual up to date information on the effects weather has on this. He will construct what is called an age stand. It is necessary to construct two – one in the open, subjected to the elements and a protected one as the control in the experiment.

All that is required is two identical patches of prepared ground each measuring three metres by three metres. What is placed in the age stands depends upon the environment that is being studied and for what the tracker is preparing. The following is a list of items that could be included:
- Materials to make a small fire
- Cigarette butt
- Animal fur, wool
- Matches used and unused
- A slice of bread
- A handful of rice
- New coin
- Empty tin cans – both acid and alkali containers

- A sweet still in its wrapper
- Small pile of animal droppings appropriate to the area
- Newspaper
- Magazine – glossy paper
- A candle
- A small amount of seed
- Thin green saplings
- Dry sticks
- Shavings from a freshly cut stick
- Pile of leaves
- Pile of pine needles
- Sapling cut in half
- Animal and human prints (which will be added after the stands have been constructed)

I have found the following procedure the best to adopt when constructing the age stands:

1 When you come to constructing the fires (remember everything is duplicated) make a small circle about 30 cm in diameter with stones about the size of your fist. Do not use man-made stones as they can explode when heated. Then add your tinder, dry grass, small dry sticks, paper etc. kindling and fuel.

2 Light the fires at the same time, using more than one match. Blow the matches out when burnt halfway down the stem. Leave the matches just outside the stone circle. Next to these used matches place several unused matches.

3 Light a cigarette, place it on the stand and leave it to burn down. This is included in the age stand in case the tracker comes across the remains of cigarettes left by the enemy.

4 Light the candle and let it burn for five to ten minutes.

5 Keeping the leaves on, bend the saplings and stick them in the ground – three saplings about 30 cms in length.

6 Snap in half a couple of dry sticks, making sure not to damage the small, fine, fibrous hairs, and place them on the stand.

7 Plant the seed as per the instructions on the packet

8 Footprints – dig a small patch in the stand to accommodate a footprint of a bare foot and a booted foot. Make an impression with the bare foot and the booted foot in the soft soil, withdrawing the foot carefully.

9 Spoor – as for 8 above, but use a plaster cast to make the imprint (see Chapter Twenty-Four) or a compliant pet.

The age stand protected from the elements is to be laid out in the same way as the first stand but protected by overhead cover. It is up to the individual what materials are used in the construction of the sheltered stand, so long as it has a roof and plenty of ventilation. The ideal procedure is as follows:

1 Make sure that the back of the stand is pointing into the prevailing wind.

2 Drive two stakes into the ground three metres apart, making sure that you leave at least one metre of each stake above the ground.

3 Strap, nail, or tie a cross-section just over three metres long across and on top of the two stakes.

4 Before going any further, assemble the items that are going into this age stand and lay them out exactly in the same way as you have done in the first age stand and light the fire.

5 Once the fire is out, place the roofing material on top of the frame so that you end up with a slanting roof. Make sure that the roof is secured with something heavy, or tied, but not nailed down. It has to be easily removable so that the sign can be inspected.

The stage is now set. With continual inspection of the stand over the next few days, weeks, months, and even years, and by keeping a log of the changes, the tracker is able to build up a reference work for his area for judging the age of sign.

Being able to assess the age of sign is a vital tool of the professional tracker. It saves him hours of frustrating effort, as he avoids being misled by foul tracks. With the application of the techniques above he can take much of the guess work out of assessing age and this, coupled with the skills depicted in the next chapter, will provide a tracker with an ability to extract the maximum information from the sign left by his quarry.

CHAPTER FIFTEEN

Deductive Skills

Deduction is the final phase of the mental process which the tracker employs. To recap, the full process is:

OBSERVE

REMEMBER

SELECT AND ANALYSE

DEDUCE AND COMPREHEND

The tracker observes and remembers. He selects and collates the relevant facts and analyses the interplay of the observations he has remembered. From this analysis he arrives at deductions about what has happened. From these deductions he gains an overall understanding and comprehension of the track picture.

When the tracker arrives at the start of the pursuit the quarry is like a ghost, without substance, but after a while the tracker not only fleshes him out, but clothes him and eventually determines his emotional state.

A couple of tales from antiquity will illuminate the thought processes which the tracker should try to cultivate. These stories are from Judea and show the application of reasoning upon observed facts – not only has the tracker to look but he has to see.

The first:

Two men were reduced to slavery on Mount Carmel. Their captor, following behind, overheard one of them telling the other, 'The camel that went before us is blind in one eye, is laden with two skin bottles, one containing wine and the other oil, and is driven by two men, one an Israelite and the other a Gentile.'

'You stiff-necked people,' cried the captor, 'how do you know all this?' They replied, 'The grass is nibbled on one side of the road only. The drops of wine on one side are sunk into the ground; whereas the oil drops remain above it. One of the drivers has relieved nature at some distance from the road, the other (according to Gentile indecency) on the road.'

The second:

The story is told of a man who bought a servant to accompany him on his journey home. Having paid the money, he discovered to his dismay that the servant was blind in one eye. 'Be comforted,' said the dealer, 'though he is blind in one eye he can see much better than persons who have two.'

The man departed with his servant. When they had gone a little way, the one-eyed slave said, 'Master, there is a traveller ahead of us. If we go fast enough we shall overtake him.'

'I see no traveller,' said the master.

'No,' said the slave, 'but I know that he is just four miles distant.'

'You are mad,' said the master. 'How can you know what passes at so great a distance, when you can scarcely see what lies before you?'

'I am not mad,' said the slave, 'moreover, the traveller is accompanied by an ass, who, like myself, is blind in one eye. She is big with young and is laden with two skin bottles, one of which contains vinegar and the other wine.' The master, who thought the slave was either insane or making fun of him, was wild with rage.

They travelled on, however, and after a time overtook the traveller, when the master found that everything was as the slave had predicted, and asked him to explain how he could know all this without seeing.

The slave replied, 'Although I have not seen what I described, yet I knew the traveller was four miles ahead of us, for the almost imperceptible impressions of the ass's hoofs in the road indicated that she was at least that distance or the impression would have been more distinct, and could not be farther or they would not have been visible. The grass, having been eaten away at one side of the path and not the other, plainly showed that the ass must have been blind in the one eye. Again, the impression which the animal left on the sand when she rested showed clearly that she was with young. Further, the impression which the liquids made on the sand, some appeared spongy while others were full of small bubbles caused by fermentation. These clearly indicated the nature of the liquids.'

To put what may have seemed a mystical and baffling process into perspective I propose to give some solid, practical cases which will convince the student that the thought processes of tracking are a part and parcel of the totality.

DEDUCTIONS FROM A SINGLE PRINT

A single print can give a whole range of information about the quarry:

- The size of a footprint gives an indication as to height
- The depth of the impression, all other things being equal, is in direct relationship to the weight of the man and his equipment
- The angle of the print with respect to the line of march is indicative of the posture of the person – an athletically built person tends to walk with his feet parallel
- Any scuff marks around the edges would suggest an idiosyncratic gait
- The footwear itself will lead to other deductions based upon its manufacture, style, and state of repair – such as the country of origin, and socio-economic group

DEDUCTIONS FROM A SERIES OF PRINTS

A series of prints from the same quarry lets the tracker judge:

- The speed
- The gait
- The load being carried – the heavier the load the shorter the pace

See Chapter Twenty-One for more details.

ESTIMATING NUMBERS IN A GROUP

A group of humans over ten will automatically leave such a well defined track that following it will present no real difficulties at all. The estimation of the numbers in a large group can only be made with any degree of accuracy when either a resting place or an overnight camp or bivouac area has been located and the individual resting places counted.

When estimating the size of smaller groups follow the track to soft ground, then take what would be an extra large step – see figure 30. Now make two lines across the track, one line level with the back of the heel of your rear leg and one level with the toes of your leading foot. Remember the unit of comparison ordinarily adopted is that of a normal walking pace. Now count every variation of footwear or part of the visible impressions left by footwear within the space between our two lines (our extra large step). Having counted the prints divide by 2 and if the result is an odd number, say 7, then the estimate is 3 or 4 people. If the estimate is an even number, say 8, then the answer is 4 people. You might be able to confirm this number by counting the different types of footwear within our extra large step. If tracking children under the age of ten, halve the extra large step and carry out the same drill as for adults.

There is a possibility of an inaccuracy if the first person to move through the soft ground weighed, say, 80 pounds and had small feet, whilst the average weight of the people in the group was, say, 160 pounds. The first person's prints could be completely obliterated. This problem can be overcome by repeating the process whenever soft ground is encountered.

By counting from the extra large step (figure 30) we get 12 impressions of footwear, partial or whole. Using our formula this gives us an estimate of 6 people. However, from figure 31 we can see that only five people made the track. A closer look at our extra large step will reveal that it is out of proportion to the average length of each step made by the group – it is nearly the distance of two steps. The Adjusted Method gauges the average distance of each step. Then we take an extra large step based on our assessment of the average. In this case the adjusted extra large step is smaller than our original one and is more in proportion to those of the group we are tracking. Our new calculations arrive at the figure of 10 footprints (whole or partial) which, when divided by 2, gives the correct answer.

As always, when we produce estimates we try and confirm as and when the opportunity arises.

ANALYSIS OF GROUPS

Study figure 32 opposite. A total of 12 prints will be observed within the extra large step. Four canine prints equals one dog. Four juvenile prints, divide by 4 (because we have taken an extra large step based on an adult pace) equals one child. Four adult

Figure 30   The extra large step method

Figure 31   The adjusted extra large step method

Figure 32   A Sunday outing

prints, divide by 2, equals 2 adults. On further examination of the human prints we can deduce the sex of the adults. The print pattern has indicated one dog walking beside an adult male – probably on a lead. On the other side of the adult male is an adult female besides her a child – because of the eveness of the child's pace most probably holding hands with the adult female. The picture is that of a family going for a walk.

By careful analysis of the prints in a group one can work out the order in which they were walking. First of all pair off the sets of prints into left and rights. Then concentrate on the prints of the quarry and see how many of the others make foul sign over its prints at any stage. For example, if there were eight in the group, walking in single file, and the set that you had isolated was fouled by three of the others, he must have been marching at number five in the group.

THE ANALYSIS OF PERIPHERALS

Apart from the quarry's footfalls his passage through the tracking medium is indicated by sign left by his equipment and clothing, for example:

- Scuff marks on trees from load-carrying equipment
- Impressions left by items of equipment such as weapons
- Marks from a walking stick
- Discarded items of equipment and rubbish
- His urine and faeces
- Fires and cooking places
- Sleeping places
- Prayer stations

Figure 33 depicts an overnight stop by a patrol. Figure 34 shows the same area after the man has departed and reveals:

(a) Weapon butt print and scuff marks

(b) Cigarette ends

(c) Marks from hammock cords on both trees

(d) Rubbish pit, halal ration wrappers

(e) Prayer mat marks, facing Mecca

(f) Scorch marks from a Tommy Cooker

(g) Scuff marks and heel marks where the person sat under the tree

(h) Marks where load-carrying equipment was placed

(i) Area used as toilet, urine marks on tree

All the above should be actively searched for by the tracker as they will provide vital evidence to indicate the following:

- Nationality
- Health
- Diet
- Morale
- Customs
- Traditions
- Religion
- Military/Civilian

The importance and the amount of information that can be deduced from a track can be seen by the importance the military

Figures 33&34 An overnight stop by a patrol

place on a tracker's report. They expect to be able to assess the following from a tracker's observations:

- Direction of movement
- Age of the track
- Numbers in the group
- The speed
- Loads
- Tactics
- Weapons
- Sex

THE MILITARY PROCESS

When the military apply the deductive process to the work of their trackers they use the following system:

- Facts – something which is physically present
- Interpretation ⎫
- Deduction   ⎬ the tracker's reasoning
- Assumption   ⎭
- Reaction – this is to the conclusions from above
- Confirmation of the reasoning and the reaction
- Reporting of the sightings
- Recording – this is the final stage of the process when the written report is submitted

INTER-DEDUCTION

Interpretation and deduction, inter-deduction in tracking terminology, is the essence of the tracker's mental processes. The tracker starts by making a list of all known facts. He then asks himself:

- How did it occur?
- Why is it like it is?
- When did it happen?
- Who caused the sign?

He then lists all the deductions from this questioning.

The tracker then brings into play his insight and imagination and makes assumptions, but he is careful to distinguish this purely mental process from the facts provided by the sign. With these assumptions the tracker is trying to anticipate the quarry's actions, not only to find the next sign but also to produce an overall track picture.

Sketch map of an incident at grid: 163348

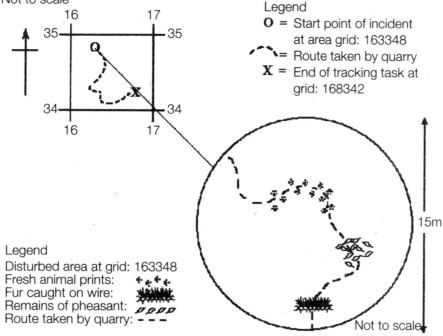

Not to scale

Legend
O = Start point of incident
at area grid: 163348
= Route taken by quarry
X = End of tracking task at
grid: 168342

15m

Not to scale

Legend
Disturbed area at grid: 163348
Fresh animal prints:
Fur caught on wire:
Remains of pheasant:
Route taken by quarry: - - -

Figure 35   Sketch map of an incident

Confirmation is the verification of the tracker's inter-deduction and assumptions. It could be the sighting of conclusive sign, such as a boot print known to be worn by enemy troops, discarded material known to belong to enemy troops, or the actual sighting of the enemy.

The table on page 150 is a rural case study which will highlight the subtleties and prove how much can be elicited from the facts when they are correctly analysed.

From the above it is assumed that at least two foxes, possibly a vixen and cub due to the two different sizes of prints and (consider the time of year vixens give birth), were out on a foraging mission and made a kill at grid 163348. They were probably disturbed by you, the tracker, which explains the very fresh sign at the incident area, and, considering the mother's instinct to protect her cub, headed for home.

To enable you, the tracker, to use any information gained, it is

Serial	Fact	Inter-Deduction
1 a	At grid 163348 the following were found: Four sets of fresh prints in the mud. Two sets smaller than the other two sets.	At least two animals, possibly dogs or foxes.
b	Considerable amount of disturbance to an area approximately 5 m² around what appears to be the remains of a pheasant – feathers and uncongealed blood.	Quarries may have made a fresh kill – blood not yet clotted. Suggesting a very fresh track only five minutes old. Possibly with visual contact.
c	Fur caught up on barbed wire 10 m south of incident area where the sign entered a wood.	A close examination of hair left behind revealed that it was definitely that of a fox.
2 a	At grid 167342 the following were located: A strong odour was smelt blowing into the area from the south.	The strength of the scent lingering in the immediate area would suggest that the quarry, in this case a fox, was in close proximity.
b	Numerous fox runs found in the area with well padded down paths superimposed by many scratch, and paw marks.	Sign indicating an area that is used by more than two foxes, possibly a foxes' earth.
c	Approximately 50 m due north numerous fox earths were found. Outside the earth an array of articles were found: animal bones, fur, feathers, dried blood, foot prints, bedding and a large area, approximately 30–40 m, of flattening and the odour of a fox.	From areas of flattening and the great array of sign lying about, the earths were used by more than two foxes.

important that you compile a report during and after a tracking task so that you can build up a log about the animals that are in your area. This log should be supported with any sketches, photographs, and specimens that it is responsible to take from the countryside.

This chapter should be read in conjunction with Chapter Twenty-One which gives more examples of how the deductive process helps the tracker.

As we saw with the two stories at the beginning of this chapter, there is nothing new in the world, and certainly the only aspect that is new in tracking is your personal development. This can be enhanced with practice, the study of tracking scenarios and the exchange of ideas with like-minded people.

CHAPTER SIXTEEN

The Lost Track Drill

Trackers are human, no matter how magical the skills may seem to the uninitiated. And because they are human, they are fallible and at some stage, however experienced a tracker is, he will lose the track. At this point he falls back on to the procedures laid down in this chapter. They will assist him to re-establish the pursuit again.

When a tracker is acquiring his skills he must always be conscious of two important facts. Firstly, losing a track can be a simple matter of taking only one or two steps in the wrong direction. And secondly, human nature will compel us to go on when there is no track and to fool ourselves into seeing a track where none exists.

LAST DEFINITE SIGN

As explained in Chapter Twelve, the Track Pursuit Drill has been evolved to assist the visual tracker in following a track made by the quarry. The corollary of this is that it prevents him losing the track and there was an emphasis laid upon the importance of noting and remembering the last definite sign, and whether it was conclusive or substantiating. The tracker must always be able to locate this last sign and may often have to orientate himself by some definite mark in its vicinity, such as a tree stump, a large stone, a prominent bush or a fence post which he can use as a reference point to re-establish his last contact with the quarry.

The last definite sign is the crux of the Lost Track Drill and therefore I think it is worth mentioning a simple technique which you can use to help you keep sight of it. I find that if I am tracking in a relatively flat, featureless area it is useful to mark the last definite sign by a short thin stick which I carry in my day pack. You may, depending on the situation, tie a brightly coloured piece of cloth to the end.

The Lost Track Drill is broken down into the following stages:

- Initial search
- Initial probe
- Initial cast
- Extended cast
- Streamline search
- Likely areas searches

THE INITIAL SEARCH (**Figure 36**)

1 From your last definite sign assess the general direction your quarry was last travelling in.

2 Describe a half circle of approximately one metre radius. Scan it from left to right and right to left. Look in the distance, the middle distance, and the foreground. Do this from the standing, kneeling and prone positions. Use a magnifying glass if necessary at this stage to identify sign that you might otherwise miss with the naked eye.

3 If you locate sign at any stage whilst carrying out the initial search, confirm that it is your quarry's by following it up a few metres. If you are happy that you are following the right track, carry on with the track pursuit drill.

4 If no track is located by use of the initial search you will now have to resort to the initial probe.

Notes:

Figure 36 The initial search

- The initial search may take up to thirty minutes
- Your movements should be limited to those necessary to fully observe the area

THE INITIAL PROBE (Figure 37)

1 From your last definite sign, probe forward to the left, front, and right. In each case only moving four to five metres maximum.

2 Every time you draw a blank retrace your steps back to your last definite sign and probe again in a different direction.

3 The techniques carried out in the initial search above should come into effect on each probe.

4 If you locate sign at any stage whilst carrying out the initial probe, confirm that it is your quarry's by following it up a few metres. If you are happy that you are following the right sign, carry on with the track pursuit drill.

5 If no track has been located after completion of the initial probe, you carry on to the next stage, the initial cast.

Notes:
- The initial probe may take up to one hour
- A visual tracker must always remember his individual signs and should never move more than three to four metres beyond a definite sign of the quarry without another definite sign in front of him
- If no sign is located you must return to the last definite sign and start again

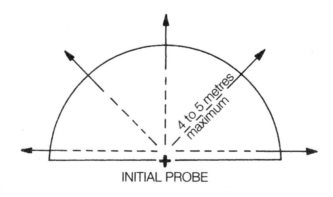

INITIAL PROBE

Figure 37   The initial probe

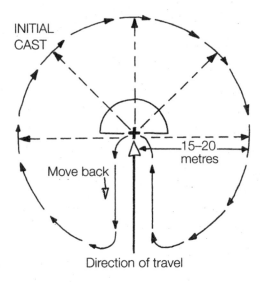

INITIAL
CAST

15–20
metres

Move back

Direction of travel

Figure 38   The initial cast

THE INITIAL CAST (**Figure 38**)

1 From your last definite sign move back along the track in the direction you have come approximately fifteen to twenty metres.

2 Begin walking in a circle fifteen to twenty metres in diameter, using the last definite sign as the centre of the circle.

3 Whether you move off to the right or left is optional. You will find that you will be influenced by the general direction of the quarry you are following, the ground, and in what direction you think you would be more likely to pick up the quarry's track again.

4 Your aim here is to cut the quarry's track. If you come across the quarry's track you must confirm that it is the same track that you have originally been following by checking the age of the new track. You then check visually backwards to ensure that the track connects up with your last definite sign. Finally, inspect forward a few paces to ensure that it is not a dead end.

5 After confirming that you have located your quarry's sign, complete the circle. The reason for completing the circle is in case another animal of the same species has passed through the circle, in which case you would have to determine which is the quarry's sign, taking into consideration all the features of sign such as age, size of print, length of stride and depth of print.

6 If you still have not located the quarry's sign on your return to your last definite sign you now have to carry out the extended cast.
Notes:

- The time taken to carry out the initial cast may be up to one hour, depending on your tracking ability, the ground, and tracking conditions, that is, the weather, time of day, age of tracks, and changes in the environment.

THE EXTENDED CAST (Figure 39)
1 The drill for the extended cast is the same as for the initial cast but this time you go back fifty to a hundred metres using the last definite sign as the centre.
Notes:

- Although the above stages have been time-consuming, up to four hours in certain cases, you will now have to accept that you will have to remain in the area and move on to the final stages of the Lost Track Drill which encompasses the searches
- Before the commencement of the next procedure you will need a rest – don't forget tracking is a very tiring process because of the concentration that it demands from the tracker, along with the physical strains. Therefore stop, have a brew, put your feet up for an hour and relax

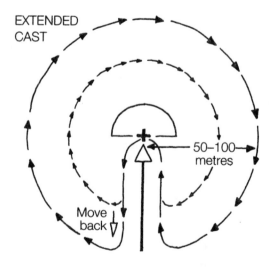

Figure 39   The extended cast

All the methods discussed so far of trying to locate the quarry's track have started at the last definite sign. The searches do not. You are now using your powers of deduction and reason to select areas you suspect the quarry will have visited in the hope that you will pick up the trail anew.

THE STREAMLINE SEARCH **(Figure 40)**
1 This is the most widely used type of search but it is only a specific type of search. It is used for two reasons:
- Animals need water
- The ground around water courses tends to be a good medium for the preservation of sign

2 Assess the general direction in which your quarry was last travelling. If using a map, do a map study with the intention of locating any water on your axis of travel and forward of your present location.

3 Whether the amount of water and its distance from your position makes it a viable water source for the quarry depends on the species. For large animals – humans, deer, badgers, and foxes – you will be studying your map for water supplies up to a distance of five kilometres. For smaller species you may be searching closer and considering much smaller supplies of water.

Figure 40   Streamline search

And for all quarry don't overlook water sources which are not mapped, such as, ditches and cow troughs.

4 If you locate a water source from your map which you think is worth searching go through the map-reading procedures as detailed in Chapter Twenty – locate your position on the ground, set your compass, and navigate to the intended location of the search.

5 If you are searching a water course the following system is the most efficient:

    a On reaching the bank of the waterway use your map to confirm you are in the right place – remember that not all waterways are marked on the map.

    b Decide in which direction you are going to follow the river and for how far. You must avoid retracing your steps and making unnecessary sign. Make a plan in your head and stick to it.

    c Check out the obvious first, that is, did the quarry go straight across the stream?

    d Before entering the stream, check the ground to ensure that any sign does not indicate that the quarry came out at your entry point.

    e Do a limited search – twenty to thirty metres of both banks, and in both directions to ascertain if there is an exit point.

6 The tracker has then to bring into play his knowledge of the sign associated with water courses:

    a Remember to check the water for discoloration. If the quarry went up stream there is a possibility that debris, sand, leaves and sticks will have been disturbed and floated downstream.

    b The overhanging branches will certainly have a high water content and therefore they will be soft thus making it easy for the bark to be scraped off and marked – look out for these indications.

    c If it is a clear water stream and the bottom is visible, it is still possible to track. Move along slowly, looking for impressions of prints, and disturbed stones (practice and familiarisation will enable trackers to recognise the natural position of stones lying on a stream bed), lack of sticks and other vegetation wedged or caught by the stones and boulders of the stream bed.

d Disturbed overhanging vegetation and the lack of spiders' webs across narrow streams will indicate the passage of some animal – this is not conclusive sign.

e All river banks are of soft soil and will certainly mark or crumble under the weight of a quarry exiting, often leaving foot impressions, skid or slide marks.

f Any quarry exiting from a stream will certainly leave two telltale signs behind – water drops which have drained off in the immediate area of its exit (the age of the track and the weather will significantly affect these) and, depending on the bottom of the stream, there will be transferred material – sand, mud, or gravel.

g The tracker checking up or down stream should look out for overhanging branches because if they are near to the water they present an obstacle and anything passing under or over them will undoubtedly leave some sign.

7 On coming across small tributaries (see figure 40) you should go along the bank fifty to a hundred metres, then cross, and go back down the other side until you hit the main river again.

LIKELY AREAS SEARCHES

In this strategy we are trying to get into the skin of the quarry and predict what he will do next and where. This is where building up the track picture in your mind's eye is so important.

The following factors should be considered:

- The possible task and intentions of the quarry
- The age of the track and the time of day when the quarry was at the place where the track has been lost – remember it will eventually get dark and you may have to abandon the track
- Consider the weather conditions which will have affected the sign – this depends on the age of the sign and therefore the tracker must have been monitoring weather conditions

The types of areas which give the best results are:

- Areas of likely camp sites or, in the case of animals, likely living areas such as dens and setts
- Steep gradients
- Track junctions

- The sides of tracks, rivers and roads
- Any other areas you feel your particular quarry may have gone

FINALLY

The aim of the Lost Track Drill is to assist you, the tracker, to relocate the track. You must remember where your last definite sign is and you must carry out the drills properly to ensure that you have not been bluffing yourself. If the sign is not located during the initial probe, then it is very likely that the quarry's last definite sign may be further back along the track. This is why the initial cast drill best assists you in re-locating the quarry's sign.

When following your quarry, avoid at all times stepping on your quarry's prints. In the case of small animals walk parallel to them; with humans and larger animals you can walk between their prints. The last thing you want when you lose the track and you have to go back to your last definite sign is to find your own footprint or those of a companion on top of your last definite sign.

Continually ask yourself the question – What would I do if I were in his position? But to be able to do this you must have developed the track picture so that you are aware of his general intentions and condition. This applies as much for an animal as it does for a man because the animal tracker has an acute appreciation of his quarry's habits which enables him to predict its movements.

We can lose a track through lack of concentration just as much as through the lack of sign and it is this mental aspect which is worth considering:

> *Tracking is tiring*
> *Don't bluff*
> *Think like the quarry*

PART THREE

Advanced Skills

CHAPTER SEVENTEEN

Training Trackers

You will already be aware that many sections of this book are specifically geared towards helping an individual who has a training role or responsibility. Where material is germane to a particular subject, such as, stalking or observation, I have left it with that chapter. What you will find here are aids to tracker training in general and to the advancement of tracking skills.

The layout of this book can be used as a general guide as to the order in which the subjects are taught.

With some groups and audiences it may be necessary to stimulate interest in a practical and spectacular way by trying to follow the tracks of something which is alive; but even then the preliminary stages of mental training, the training of the senses, stalking and so on should be taken up as soon as possible. If habits of observation are not formed, the potential tracker's keenness on tracking will soon fizzle out as he becomes frustrated with continually losing the track.

The student has to be shown that the subject is a great deal deeper and more complex than he might at first think. But if he is led through the skills progressively by an enthusiastic instructor and the lessons are put across in an interesting way it will be an encouraging challenge and not a daunting task.

For example, if you ask the potential tracker to follow the track of a motorcar on a soft dirt-road, he will be able to follow it for half a mile with very little difficulty, but if you ask him to follow the track of a man across hard stony ground, he will lose it in under twenty-five metres. The training has to lie somewhere between these two extremes.

I am alive to the danger of accepting literature as a good substitute for actual practice and, as with most things which are worth doing, tracking isn't easy and continual practice is necessary. Trackers think like trackers and see sign where the uninitiated don't: any environment is rich in sign to the senses of a tracker – the environment in which we live should not deter us from practising the lessons. Having said this, there are tracking situations which are more suitable for the novice than others – snow, mud and wet sand are ideal tracking mediums. And often the best time to practise is first thing in the morning when there is an abundance of fresh sign.

This chapter is directed at any person who finds himself with the responsibility of running training for trackers. There are the traditional groups such as:

- The military NCO of a recce or a special forces unit
- The rural police force – especially the scene of crimes specialists
- The teacher or group leader with a remit covering outdoor pursuits – Scout leaders

But there are other bodies who will find it beneficial to study tracking in a structured fashion and therefore utilise the skills of a tracking instructor:

- Conservationists
- Bird watchers
- Protectors of endangered species
- Gamekeepers
- Farmers with a threat of rustlers
- Mountain rescue volunteers

TRACKING EXERCISES AND LESSONS

First of all I will list the types of exercises and make a few observations. After that I will give a set of detailed instructions for each one.

The following are the main types of tracking exercises and instructional periods that I have used in the past to train military trackers:

- Observation stand
- Observation lane
- Age stand
- Pace tracking exercise
- Pace tracking lane
- Incident awareness stand
- Incident awareness lane
- Tracking competition
- Final exercise

The list above is in the order in which these activities should take place to gain the maximum benefit. The introduction to the age stand and the importance of being able to judge the age of sign has to be brought to the student's notice before he attempts the pace tracking lane.

In order to make the exercises and lessons a success, the instructor has to plan meticulously and the following details are given as an aid to that end. Firstly, there are some general considerations which must be covered with regards to any exercise or lesson.

The following list gives the main administrative details which have to be covered to ensure that any exercise runs smoothly:

- Obtain permission to use any land
- Carry out a full rehearsal of the exercise
- Compose a full list of equipment required of the instructor and of the students
- Issue a warning order giving the assembly time and place and what equipment the students need to have with them
- State the aim of the exercise
- Be aware of the students' details – numbers, age, experience
- Consider timings – travel time to the exercise area, duration of exercise
- Organise transport, meals, wet weather clothing, maps, equipment, alternative programme in case of the exercise having to be postponed (transport breakdowns, misty weather during an observation exercise)
- Prepare a detailed set of instructions for any assistants and for the students

OBSERVATION STAND

This exercise is similar to the one used by the Royal Marines which I referred to in Chapter Seven under the section 'Some Exercises for Youth Leaders'. Here I will describe the method of laying out the stand and conducting the exercise.

First of all make a list of the items which you intend to use in the observation stand. Then, having selected the piece of ground, mark out the left and right of arc and the foreground, middle

OBSERVATION STAND LAYOUT

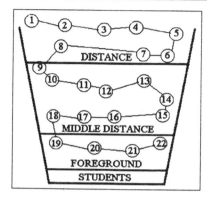

1	Rucksack	9	Person with dog	17	Watch
2	Jacket	10	Belt	18	Packet of crisps
3	Fishing rod	11	Shoe	19	Handbag
4	Cap or hat	12	Football	20	Pencil or pen
5	School bag	13	Tent	21	Loose change
6	Push bike	14	Notebook – magazine	22	Conclusive sign
7	Bike pump	15	Jumper		
8	Person	16	Radio		

POINTS TO NOTE
- All items should be listed and laid out in a sequence so that you do not lose any.
- Instructor's sketch map will not be numbered until he gets on the ground and lays the equipment out as he may change his mind about the placement of the items.
- The kit list is only a guide. Put out what you think the students will get the most benefit from.

Figure 41   Observation stand layout

distance and far distance using broad tape similar to that used to demarcate hazards around building sites.

Make a sketch of the observation stand area. Position yourself where the students will be and then direct your assistant to lay out the items, starting from the far distance and working back towards where you are. Accurately record on your sketch where the items are.

Indicate from which position in the viewing area they can be seen and whether the observer has to be standing, kneeling or lying. You also note why each item can be seen – shape, shine, shadow, spacing, silhouette and movement.

When everything is ready for the students call them forward and brief them fully about the limits of the area which they are expected to observe and their limits of movement, that is within the viewing area only. Give the students a copy of the bare sketch map, or they can be expected to produce their own, depending on the time available and the training carried out up to this point. Inform the group that they will have to move about within the viewing area and adopt various positions to see all the items. Tell them what is required of them: they must place each item on the sketch map, describe it, and give a distance to it. Remind them to put their names on their papers, that referring or talking is not allowed, that they have five minutes to tune in, then set them a time limit, and inform them that they will be given a ten and five minute warning to indicate the approaching end of their allotted time.

After the test collect in the papers and, in conjunction with your partner, indicate to the students, starting from the distance, where and what the items are. Remember this part of the exercise is an important part of the learning process, so don't rush it. The usual method is that the assistant stands behind the item and he then points to it. If there are students who still cannot see it they are encouraged to change stance, to move and to carry out the figure of eight search with their eyes around the object. After a few minutes the assistant slowly lifts the item. It is convenient if the first item is a rucksack or a bag so that the rest can be stowed in it as they are collected.

As with any training, gradually build up the confidence of the students by keeping the standard within their grasp.

A careful analysis of the papers is then required to determine the areas for each student that need attention. For example some will see objects because of their shape, whereas others are attracted to the shine from surfaces but are inattentive to shadow and spacing. Other students have trouble with distant objects or items which are hanging from branches.

OBSERVATION LANE

This exercise is a development of the preceding one but in this case a lane is delineated, either by tape as previously or by the bounds of an obvious track which the students are not allowed to stray from. The length of an observation lane is usually about fifty to a hundred metres. The items are outside the boundaries of the track.

The students can set off as a group or the exercise can be

OBSERVATION LANE
SKETCH MAP FOR INSTRUCTORS

1	Notebook	11	Person
2	Nature trail marker	12	Tent
3	Pair of shoes	13	Compass
4	Watch	14	Radio – on
5	Lighter	15	Nature trail marker
6	Person digging	16	Nature trail marker
7	Hat	17	Map
8	Jumper	18	Torch
9	Sleeping bag	19	Camera
10	Fire	20	Rucksack

Figure 42   Observation lane

conducted individually. Either way there should not be any conferring and, if the students are going through as individuals, those who have finished the exercise should be isolated from the others.

The debrief is as stated above very important and the same procedure as before should be used where an assistant indicates the items and the students are given a second chance to try their observational skills.

To add variety, the lane can have live aspects such as smoke from a fire, men occupying a camp, and people talking.

AGE STAND

A full description of this training technique is given in Chapter Fourteen.

PACE TRACKING EXERCISE

As was stated in the definitions in Chapter Two this is 'pace for pace' tracking carried out during the tuning in period or when the track becomes difficult to pursue.

Remember, as an instructor, select the tracking medium which is suitable to the standard of your student – mud, snow and sand for the beginner, dew-laden grass in the early morning at a later stage, leading to hard packed dry earth and rock for the accomplished student.

It will be mainly ground sign that you will be following when pace tracking and you have to start from a known quarry's sign, whether it is conclusive or substantiating sign. Then make a comprehensive study of that particular sign to gain as much information as you can – direction, size of print, width, depth, left or right foot, fore or hind in the case of an animal, sex and age. Once you have taken all these into consideration, your next task will be to find the next sign.

Let's run through an easy example, figure 43:

In this case there is a conclusive sign made by a human's right shoe (a), box 1. From your position (b) look forward from the end of your toes and the width of your body to a maximum distance of one metre.

Look to the obvious area where the left shoe should be (c).

Once you have established the next print, in this case the left shoe, place your right foot parallel to but not on the quarry's right footprint, see box 2.

Next bring your left foot forward but *do not* put it down on the ground, sweep it from left to right over the ground between the quarry's right foot (a) and the quarry's left foot (c).

Now place your left foot down between (a) and (c).

Bring your right foot forward, placing it between the quarry's left and right foot, then kneel down, see box 3.

The reason you carry out this sweep is fourfold.

Firstly, to establish the length of the quarry's pace so that you adapt your pace to suit the pace of your quarry. This enables you to anticipate where the quarry's next sign will be.

Secondly, so that you don't foul the quarry's sign by placing your foot on top of it.

Thirdly, from the kneeling position you can get a closer look at the quarry's next sign, using a magnifying glass if required.

And finally, to make sure that the quarry has not put an indicator pace in between (c) and (a) which would reveal a change of direction.

Figure 43   Pace tracking

Once you are confident that you have established where the quarry's left foot was, place your left foot beside it, see box 4.

When you have built up confidence in pace tracking you will find that you will be able to follow a quarry at a normal walking pace, see boxes 5 and 6, only carrying out the sweep when necessary.

When pace tracking always be aware of the quarry changing

direction – look for the indicator pace. Do not be tempted to jump sign as you will only loose the track and end up fouling the sign. Pace tracking means exactly that, following the track pace for pace with the tracker keeping in step pace for pace. A further point for consideration in pace tracking is the speed of the quarry. In the case of humans you should have no problem in finding out if they are walking, jogging, or running when you do the sweep.

The same principles apply to pace tracking animals but in this case measure the walk or hop of a bird with a stick and use this to locate the next print. With animals there is an added problem, a human has a reason for going from A to B and will generally go in a straight line. Animals, however, are much more unpredictable. With four-legged creatures the ideal situation would be establishing all four prints in, say, mud, snow, or sand. Usually you will be following only two or three prints and the direction may be less predictable.

The organisation of a pace tracking exercise is mainly about avoiding one group inadvertently causing foul sign for another. So to that end the instructor divides the group into two, say the red and the blue teams. Pair off each member of the red with a blue team member. Indicate a start line, for instance the edge of a bridle path, line the red team members up along the path at ten-metre intervals and have their counterparts on the blue team stand behind them back to back.

The group laying the track make a conclusive sign and plant a marker by it as the start point for their partner in the other group. They then walk off in the given direction (the instructor ensures that the tracks are parallel) for a given distance, say fifty to a hundred metres, and sit down out of sight of the tracking group who are then shown their respective first conclusive sign and are told to pace track from there.

After each track, follow it up with a lessons learnt debriefing session. The groups then change roles. The instructor should encourage the students to be slow and methodical at this stage. It is not a race. They will learn from each piece of sign and each pace if they proceed steadily.

The practice can be varied as the students improve by having the quarry group putting in indicator paces using deceptions, varying the speed, walking with a stick, or joining a group.

A pair of student trackers can carry out this exercise on their own so long as they set themselves a cut-off time if they do lose contact with each other. They can re-establish contact by whistle blasts or heading for the ERP (see 'Safety' below).

PACE TRACKING LANE

The Pace Tracking Lane is the next development in the tracker's training. The instructor chooses a piece of virgin ground, probably in a woodland area but not necessarily. He tapes off the left and right boundaries, leaving an untouched corridor one metre wide and not necessarily straight. The quarry (probably the instructor himself or his assistant) then walks the length of the corridor between the tapes. He then seals off the ends with tape.

The students then move down the boundaries of the corridor and record in their note books any observations relating to the passage of the quarry and the sign it has left. Or, if possible, the student walks down the side with the instructor and points with a stick to any sign and describes it and the deductions made from it. He tells the instructor whether the sign is conclusive or substantiating. He should be able to tell the direction of travel.

These corridors can be varied to introduce groups and men carrying equipment which brushes the vegetation.

INCIDENT AWARENESS STAND

The stimulation of interest is often best achieved, especially with sophisticated youngsters and adults, by making the training relevant to realistic situations that they are likely to encounter or to which they can relate. Incident scenarios are an invaluable tool.

The trainer of trackers can use the scenes of incidents to great effect. Not only do they add realistic variety to the training but they engage the trainees' senses, deductive powers, and their imagination as they try to get into the character of the quarry.

Some of the scenarios that I have used in the past to stimulate the grey matter of a group are:

- A road traffic accident where somebody is missing
- A mountaineering search
- A poaching incident
- A fisherman missing from the river bank

- A kidnap
- The reconstruction of a crime from the sign left on the ground, or in a room, is a good exercise for our deductive faculties, but the setter of the stage should have a very clear idea of the story he means to convey by the sign
- And, of course, any number of military and counter-terrorist scenarios, such as the site of an ambush or an attack, after which the tracker team is detailed to locate the fleeing enemy

INCIDENT AWARENESS LANE EXERCISE

The incident awareness lane is a develoment of the previous exercise which puts even more pressure upon the deductive powers of the students. The following is the administrative detail required to set one of these up.

The lane should be about 150 metres long and throughout its length the student should be able to identify about six sites. Each site should have sign which indicates an activity. The sites are to each side of the lane so that the students can observe them without fouling the sign for the next group. The following are a list of sites with the appropriate sign which should be left by the instructor:

- Rest site – cigarettes, rucksack scuff marks on trees against which they have been leant, areas where four people have

1	Rest site	5	Water halt
2	Obstacle crossing – over a log	6	Meal halt
3	First aid incident/ambush site	7	Rest site
4	Overnight stop		

Figure 44 Layout of an incident awareness lane

sat, complete with heel prints where they have been resting, urination site

- Meal halt – food remains, some of the same points as for
  the rest site
- Water replenishment site – footprints meandering around
  the area, sign where water bottles have been placed down,
  transfer of water onto other areas
- Overnight stop – four sleeping areas, knife cuts in the
  vegetation, latrine area, buried waste area, fire site
- Ambush site – vegetation bent over to produce arcs of fire,
  vegetation used to produce camouflage, flattened areas
  where they have lain
- First aid incident – after an obstacle such as a steep slope
  or a large tree across the track which had to be negotiated,
  there should be sign where a man has slipped and fallen
  and then limped away, sat down, and then been bandaged
  by a medic, some discardables from the medic pack

It should be noted that if judging the age of the sign in the
incident awareness lane exercise is one of the aspects which is
being tested, the instructor must set up the incident scenes with
this in mind to ensure that the sign and its age are compatible
with what is being depicted.

TRACKING COMPETITION

It is often a fitting finale to a tracking course to run a competition. The most effective way to organise the competition is in the
form of what we call in the military a round robin where the
students go round in small groups from event to event. The
layout is important so as to keep the students moving, and to
arrange the subjects in order of difficulty – see figure 45. The
elements which I tend to include are:

- Kim's Game – see Chapter Six
- Observation stand – see page 165
- Observation lane – see page 167
- Age stand – judging the age of sign – see Chapter Four-
  teen
- Incident awareness lane, deducing what happened at the
  site – see page 173
- Pace tracking lane – see page 172

1   Kim's Game   4   Age stand
2   Observation stand   5   Incident awareness lane
3   Observation lane   6   Pace tracking lane

Figure 45   The layout for a tracking competition

FINAL EXERCISE

The culmination to all this tracker training would be a tracking exercise which is simply a group or an individual setting off as the quarry along a route set by the instructor. They have to follow the given route so that the instructor has control over the exercise. The tracker group then attempt to follow from the given start point which will probably be an incident scenario.

I have taken part in an exercise such as this in the Malayan jungle which proceeded for five days and culminated in the tracking team locating an enemy camp and then mounting an attack on the same. The first exercises should only be six or eight hours long and can be less ambitious but to make them work the students' standard of tracking has to be of a fairly high level and the exercise needs to be well co-ordinated by the instructional team who need good communications between themselves, the quarry and the tracking team. To guarantee control, especially with an inexperienced group or over difficult terrain, one of the instructors can travel with the tracking team as an observer.

SOME PRACTICALITIES OF TRAINING TRACKERS
Safety – the emergency rally point (ERP)
So that you as an instructor can keep control of the group during outdoor exercises and training it is a good idea to instigate a procedure known as the emergency rally point (ERP).

The chief instructor designates the ERP at the start of an outdoor activity and only he can change it and if he changes it during an activity he is personally responsible for making everyone in the group aware of the location of the new ERP. It must be a point on the ground with which the group is familiar, such as the point where the transport dropped the group off, a gate in a field, a tent, or a house. The ERP is not selected from the map without confirming its physical presence.

The function of the ERP is that in an emergency or if groups become split this is where they make for. If you have the manpower one of the instructor team or an admin person is detailed to man the ERP for the duration of the activity or until everyone is accounted for.

Group size

There is a limit to the number of people one instructor can train at various stages of the tracking syllabus. With many of the classroom lessons the group is really only limited by the classroom but when we commence the practical exercises there are severe limitations. For instance, when following a trail (a track made up of sign laid for the purposes of training trackers) three students is the maximum. If there are any more the crowding causes confusion and can obliterate the sign.

Stress/pressure

I have found that the people at the back of a group of trainees see more sign than the person actually doing the tracking. The explanation for this I firmly believe is that those at the back are not under any pressure and, as a result, are more relaxed. This phenomenon of the learning process needs to be taken into account and employed beneficially by the instructor.

Stimulating interest for the younger student

Three simple means of giving practice and stimulating interest might be suggested. First, in town or country a small tracking ground out-of-doors could be carefully smoothed and different pieces of food left on it overnight. The next day the tracks that are almost certain to appear on the ground may be carefully examined. The food selected should be such as to tempt the birds and animals that are likely to frequent the locality.

Second, in the country in the winter there are many fields which are marked by the tracks of the stock in them. Each individual can be given a different set of prints and told to trace the animal. This exercise should only be undertaken provided the group do not disturb the stock itself in any way and only with the permission of the livestock owner.

Thirdly, students should be made aware that tracking does not necessarily mean following by marks upon the ground. Birds can be tracked by their calls, their plumage, their flight pattern. Birds of prey can also be located by the bones and feathers of small birds and animals that are scattered below the trees where they nest.

TRAINING TECHNIQUES

I would like to emphasise the fact that even traditional trackers undergo training – trackers are not born, they are trained. Sometimes their training takes years and is very arduous. There is a great deal to be said for absorbing a subject over a long period, as it will then become a part of the person and the skills won't disappear after a short layoff.

Training has to be progressive, moving on logically from subject to subject with breaks and revision periods designed into the programme for consolidation. Then the subjects have to be amalgamated to produce a practical skill. These skills have to be tested under realistic but controlled conditions in order to validate the instruction. By laying out tracker training in this fashion we progress and meld the skills without drab repetition. The secret of success in tracker training is to secure and sustain interest by providing variety.

The following are some of the techniques I have used in the past with civilians.

Trail as opposed to track

I am using the word trail to designate a track that is made artificially, as opposed to the track that is made by the feet of an animal, human or otherwise. This is not a correct interpretation of the word, but my difficulty is that I wish to make a distinction between the tracking of an unwitting quarry and a designed tracking exercise.

In utilising trails we work progressively from stage to stage and try to provide variety. The most elementary form of a trail is that made by scattering paper on the ground so that those behind can follow, that is to say a paper-chase. A further definite stage is reached, however, by the laying of a wool trail. Odds and ends of wool or cloth are cut up into pieces five or six centimetres long and used in place of paper. There are several benefits; by using different colours separate trails can be used for each individual more or less running along parallel lines and converging on a common point. The cloth can be placed on bushes as well as on the ground, and be tied to branches or twigs overhead, thus training in all-round observation. When we come to tracking proper we will not always find all the sign on the ground, so practice in looking up as well as down is a good thing. Obviously this sort of exercise is particularly appropriate for the younger student.

Progressive methods in this kind of trail can be utilised by scattering the material thickly at first and gradually reducing the number of pieces put down and increasing the interval between each. An important point to remember is that anything strange, say an early flower, can be brought to the notice of those following by laying a piece of cloth alongside it.

The next stage, so far as our progressive steps are concerned, is the laying of what is known as a nature trail. That is where the trail layer leaves indications. These indications can be either to supplement the sign, such as turning over a leaf, placing an oak leaf on a holly bush, breaking a twig, or, by some pre-arranged convention between the trail layer and the following groups, they can indicate direction, for instance by tying small bunches of grass together, breaking a twig and laying it in a certain direction, arranging piles of stones. Figure 46 shows some examples of trail markers.

The last stage is the introduction of sign proper and not contrived clues, such as those above. At first the signs should be made at frequent intervals and be large in size, and then distances between each sign should be increased and their size decreased. As the skill level increases deceptions can be incorporated and the tracking medium altered from easy mud and

Figure 46 Trail markers

wet sand through grass and leaf-strewn woodland to rocky terrain.

In this last stage especially anyone who is laying a trail to be followed would be wise to get another instructor to see if he can follow it before setting the potential tracker on the job. When you lay a trail yourself it seems quite easy to follow, but when you try and follow a trail laid by someone else it is not quite as easy. There is an obvious safety aspect for the adult laying such trails for young student trackers in that the trail has got to be so designed that they don't get lost even if they lose the trail.

Age stands

Age stands are fully described in Chapter Fourteen and are a necessary part of any long established tracker training unit because the judgement of the age of sign is an indispensable skill in the tracker's armoury.

Sand boxes

With the aid of this device the instructor can explain how the speed of the quarry, its weight, and any other characteristics affect the print.

So far I have just fleetingly mentioned the main stages that might be adopted in laying trails, but have not discussed the variety. The instructor's imagination is the key factor in making any training interesting.

THE YOUNG TRACKER

The following are the guidelines for young trackers and should be noted by anyone with a responsibility for training young people:

- Leave a note of your route and the expected time of return
- Ensure you have some food with you – it is difficult for anyone to concentrate if they are hungry
- Dress sensibly, wear stout footwear and clothing that does not rustle when you move
- Notice which way the wind is blowing and approach the area of suspected sign down wind
- When stalking move slowly, a few paces at a time, stop regularly and observe in all directions
- If accompanied, arrange a series of signals with your companions before you start – don't talk unless it is essential
- Make notes and sketches when it is appropriate on all that you see, as it is not easy to remember later when you come to make your report
- If you see the quarry, keep perfectly still. Don't try to get too close. Use your binoculars to see details
- If the quarry moves away, don't try and follow too soon
- As a general rule never touch or frighten away any young of the animal kingdom, if you are lucky enough to come across them. Admire from a distance and then move away very quietly
- Keep an eye on the time; remember that someone will be worried if you are late
- Carry a whistle – if you get lost, blow it at regular intervals to attract attention

- Carry a good set of binoculars
- Take all the items necessary for a successful and safe day's tracking – see below.

EQUIPMENT

There follows a suggested kit list that will assist you to carry out a tracking task successfully, safely and with relative comfort. The list will assist the beginner to be more efficient and to achieve better results when carrying out a tracking task. I myself use many of the items listed below and some that are not, reading glasses and a hearing aid – signs of middle age! The general rule for items of kit is, 'If it is of use take it,' but don't fall into the trap of dressing up like a Christmas tree. A good many trackers that I have had the privilege of being associated with have never heard of most of the items listed, never mind used them, and even if they had it wouldn't have made them any better trackers than they already were. There is no substitute for experience. Before wasting money unnecessarily on a lot of fancy kit, do some local area tracking to see if this is the hobby for you. Don't give up after a few hours, I have seen people struggling for days and then it just clicks. Remember, find an easy area to start with which has plenty of sign.

The kit list

Essentials:
- Day sack
- Suitable outdoor clothing
- Map(s) protected in a plastic bag or map case
- Torch – medium size with a switch that can't be inadvertently put on
- Silva compass
- Long tweezers
- Note book and pencil (rather than pen and keep them in a plastic bag)
- A set of lightweight waterproofs – jacket and trousers (if not already being worn)
- A short home-made flag – maximum length 0.75 metres
- Exact change for the telephone, or a phone card, or a mobile phone for use in emergencies
- Binoculars – the ideal binoculars for watching wildlife

areas is 7×50 or 8×40. Higher magnification binoculars are very difficult to hold still without a support. You may want to use them in some pretty awkward positions. For a young person whose budget is tight a pair of ex-military binoculars in good condition will suffice. These can be easily obtained from the many ex-military surplus stores

- Magnifying glass
- Cold snacks – to last a day
- Thermos flask – with a hot drink
- Water bottle
- Tape measure
- Small personal medical kit (plasters, headache tablets, insect repellent etc. – ask the advice of your local pharmacist if in doubt). Small waterproof container of plaster of Paris and the kit required to make a plaster mould
- This book in a plastic bag
- Small pen knife
- Whistle
- Watch

Optional items:
- Camera
- Tape recorder
- Mobile telephone
- Night viewing aids

Remember prior to departure:
- Inform someone of your intentions
- Lay out and check all the items you intend to take with you on your tracking task

CHAPTER EIGHTEEN

Military Tracking

Trackers in the military are used for two main purposes. The first is to gain information about the enemy and so provide useful intelligence to the commanders. The second is to locate the enemy and destroy him.

Tracking skills are also taught to many who will never become trackers, working on the principle that, if a soldier has a knowledge about how a tracker operates, it will help him evade a tracking team.

THE INTELLIGENCE GATHERING ROLE

A visual tracker must realise that gaining information starts at the beginning of a pursuit and is confirmed time and time again throughout the task. Each individual piece of sign, whether it is direction, numbers or age, is telling the tracker something about the quarry. The information gained by the tracker may be of vital use later and affect decision-making. However, all information gathered during a pursuit task will give the tracker a better understanding of the quarry and with this knowledge he will be able to counter any moves the quarry may employ.

The tracker has to establish in which direction the quarry is heading and check the map for the best route. A calculated guess can help plot the quarry's route and, if the trail is lost, this will make it easier to find. The military tracker above all others has to get into the skin of his quarry – he has to think like the enemy, so he is able to anticipate what may be deadly moves.

All the time he has to be asking himself, 'What would I do?' This will help him follow the track if it gets less obvious. There are only a few ways around an obstacle like rocks or fallen trees and a trained eye will spot these places. The place that you would use to cross a river will probably be the one that the quarry used, that is, if they are unaware of your follow-up.

If the enemy is in a hurry he will take the most direct route. It is possible to predict this and then do as the Rhodesian Selous Scouts did, place ambush teams forward. More recently colleagues of mine advised an anti-poaching unit in Botswana to try this tactic against well-armed rhino poachers – the results were fatal to the poachers.

The intelligence value of tracking is so important that the New Zealand SAS (probably the foremost military unit in tracking skills) dedicate a whole section of their tracking course to this subject. They call it Incident Awareness and the following is based upon my experiences of serving with them.

RECOGNISING AN INCIDENT SITE

The recognition of an incident site is a crucial feature as this is where information is gleaned and the track picture enhanced. Unfortunately, some sites are not obvious because of their size, their position, or the enemies' attempts to disguise it.

AIDS TO RECOGNITION OF SITES

There are some techniques which the military tracker employs to help him identify an incident site. They are:

- Anticipate incidents, for example be looking for the next camping site at about a suitable distance from the last one
- When there are changes in direction due either to the enemy looping back, breaking off the track, or where pointers indicate a more abrupt change
- Localised increases in sign
- Discardables such as food wrappers which would indicate a meal stop
- Study areas where incidents are likely to happen, such as at water resupply points, where there are obstacles to be crossed, or where halts will be taken, such as at the top of steep climbs

HELP IN FINDING A LOST TRACK

A thorough search of possible incident sites is invaluable if the target sign has been lost.

DANGERS OF INCIDENT SITES

If the enemy is alert to trackers incident sites can be used to lure the tracking party into booby trapped localities or into an area which is a registered target for their support and indirect fire weapons.

THE SEQUENCE OF EVENTS

If the following procedure is used nothing will be missed and time will not be wasted. The sequence is:

- When a potential incident site is identified move back and go into all round defence
- Plan the search which may include looping to determine the size, layout, entry and exit points
- The tracker with his cover man conduct a systematic search and record all facts on a sketch. The sketch has to include as a minimum: north, entry and exit points, positions of all sign
- Depending upon the size of the incident area the rest of the patrol can surround the perimeter or give cover from features outside the immediate area
- Briefly record the interpretations and brief the patrol commander or another tracking team if handing over
- If the incident warrants it send a track report signal to the base
- Continue with the task

The type of information and the intelligence deductions drawn from it are covered in detail in Chapter Fifteen.

OFFENSIVE ACTION TASKS

Special forces are usually trained in the arts of tracking. They then produce patrols which are a lethal combination of the primordial skills of tracking and the most technically sophisticated techniques of directing an awesome amount of accurate, long-range fire power from either ships, aircraft, or artillery. The modern special forces patrol has become a very potent mix of the ancient and modern.

But even alone a special forces tracking team can inflict damage on an enemy out of all proportion to its size because of the element of surprise which it has gained during the pursuit of an unwary or complacent enemy. The following case studies exemplify the use of trackers in an offensive mission.

In Malaysia in 1956 an Australian tracking patrol successfully followed and almost overtook a party of approximately fifteen CTs (communist terrorists). They had tracked them for over ten kilometres through jungle in eighteen hours. The team of trackers consisted of two Australian trackers, one a dog handler, an Iban tracker (brought in from neighbouring Borneo) and a local aborigine. Whenever the sign became warm the Iban and the local aborigine tracker would tend to become frightened and suddenly lose the trail. When this occurred one or both of the Australians would take over the lead and continue the track. The team commander achieved outstanding results by exploiting the peculiar composition of his team.

In the same campaign in an area only thirty miles north-west of Kuala Lumpur the SAS were involved in a protracted search and destroy mission. The unit tracked down a group of CTs over a fourteen-week period. Sergeant Bob Turnbull was one of the extraordinary group of SAS soldiers in the Malay campaign who became better at tracking than the Ibans. Others in this group were Sergeants Creighton and Hawkins. During one follow Turnbull tracked a four-man group for five days until he was able to close with them and kill them.

More recently the South African Army employed Bushmen trackers in offensive follow-up operations into Namibia. These tracking units were so offensively organised that they had their own RPG 7 and mortar sections.

EVASION

The evasion skills of my tracker training in the SAS were often put to good use on the escape and evasion exercises which were a regular part of the training cycle. Being accustomed to what creates good sign makes it a fairly straightforward task to avoid leaving an obvious track of your passage through an area.

The importance of a knowledge of tracking to a soldier's survival, especially a soldier in an unconventional unit, is highlighted by the following. These are the standing orders for Rogers' Rangers, a unit which fought the French and Indians in the days when North America was still being contested. These orders are dated 1736 and read as follows:

STANDING ORDERS – ROGERS' RANGERS
MAJOR ROBERT ROGERS

Don't forget nothing.

Have you musket clean as a whistle, hatchet scoured, sixty rounds powder and ball, and be ready to march at a minute's warning.

When you're on the march, act the way you would if you was sneaking up on a deer – see the enemy first.

Tell the truth about what you see and what you do. There is an army depending on us for correct information. You can lie all you please when you tell other folks about the Rangers, but don't lie to a Ranger or officer.

Don't never take a chance you don't have to.

When we're on the march we march single file, far enough apart so one shot can't go through two men.

If we strike swamps, or soft ground, we spread out abreast, so it's hard to track us.

When we march, we keep moving till dark, so as to give the enemy the least possible chance at us.

When we camp, half the party stays awake the other half sleeps.

If we take prisoners, we keep 'em separate till we have had time to examine them, so they can't cook up a story between 'em.

Don't ever march home the same way. Take a different route so you won't be ambushed.

No matter whether we travel in big parties or little ones, each party has to keep a scout twenty yards ahead, twenty yards on each flank, and twenty yards in the rear, so the main body can't be surprised and wiped out.

Every night you'll be told where to meet if surrounded by a superior force.

Don't sit down to eat without posting sentries.

Don't sleep beyond dawn. Dawn's when the French and Indians attack.

Don't cross a river by a regular ford.

If somebody's trailing you, make a circle, come back onto your own tracks, and ambush the folks that aim to ambush you.

Don't stand up when the enemy's coming against you. Kneel down, lie down, hide behind a tree.

Let the enemy come till he's almost close enough to touch. Then let him have it and jump out and finish him up with your hatchet.

The above may make graphic reading today but the awareness of the tracker's skills are implicit in many of the rules and were reiterated in more modern prose by the SAS so that they could evade and survive in the jungles of Malaya and Borneo. Their rules for 'Lead Scouts and Jungle Soldiers' run to thirty points and mention sign and the tracker's skills many times, as you can see below.

LEAD SCOUTS AND JUNGLE SOLDIERS

1 Do not 'sign post' your routes. Laid down tactics will determine whether all camp rubbish is to be buried or carried out.

2 Keep yourself fit, your weapon clean and your equipment ready at all times.

3 Always move with stealth and never at such a speed that your presence in the area is telegraphed ahead of your visible distance.

4 Your life and the lives of others often depends on the intelligence and 'info' that you gain and pass on. State clearly whether your information is fact, deduction, assumption or an intelligent guess. Never lie or knowingly pass on false information.

5 Physical fitness is a personal responsibility, but even a fit and alert Scout can get tired. Never 'bash on' when you are so tired that you find your concentration and alertness slipping.

6 Never look at the ground while moving forwards.

7 When faced with thick undergrowth, if possible go around. If you have to go through, weave your way under or over. Never cut or allow your pack or body to get caught up in the branches or vines and so cause sounds and movement at the tops of young trees.

8 Remember that the sound made by the rattle from poorly packed equipment, unnecessary talking above a whisper, a cough or a broken stick, will travel outwards in all directions. Don't alert and warn an enemy in the area of your

presence and approach, thus giving him time to come into the aim before you could possibly spot his movement.

9 When acting as a Lead Scout for a patrol, ensure that your cover man is always a tactical distance away from you.

10 Never forget your own 'sign' leaving tendency; ground sign, top sign, and the phantom twig snapper. If necessary detail tail end Charlie to brush over and camouflage your tracks. Always consider the possibility of using deception tactics.

11 Always vary your route and timings, out and back from all patrols; unless you want to be ambushed.

12 Patrol with, visit with, eat with, sit with and sleep with your weapon at all times. Never let it out of your sight or further than arm's length away from you.

13 'Belt order' will contain your survival equipment, together with other laid down items. Wear your belt order at all times and have it at arm's length whilst asleep.

14 Always remember that as the Lead Scout, it is your responsibility to ensure that you do not lead your patrol into the killing zone of an enemy ambush. Make use of the 'listening halts'. Develop all your senses to a high pitch and if ever you become suspicious of the area ahead, stop the patrol and have a 'listening halt' or go forward and check it out with your cover man. Look through not at the vegetation and undergrowth to the second or third layer.

15 Observe and become familiar with the natural, sights and smells of the insect world, the animal kingdom, the bird life and all forms of vegetation in your area of operations. Be alert to any sign, which indicates man's presence in the area.

16 Once on patrol 'switch on' and stay 'switched on' for the complete duration of the patrol. Move with stealth and with every man spaced out at the correct tactical distance; cross all obstacles tactically and ensure that all halts; the smoke halt; the meal halt; the water halt; the listening halt; the radio comms halt; the navigational check halt and the overnight bivouac halt are carried out in a tactical manner.

17 Ensure that you are familiar and well practised in all RV (rendez-vous) drills and procedures.

18 Approximately one hundred yards before stopping for a meal halt, leave a drop-off man to check rear. This could be the second Scout. Before commencing the meal halt, check up to a hundred yards outwards and forwards of area to ensure you are not beside an enemy location. This would be the Lead Scout's job. Front, rear and all round security must always be maintained both while on the move and during all halts.

19 Well disciplined and immediate reactions on contact with, or on coming under fire from the enemy, can often result in a routed foe.

20 Always be aware of the patrols mission, be familiar and well practised in all contact drills. On occasions it may be necessary to avoid contact and let the enemy go by, then reporting his presence and activities rather than getting involved in a 'fire fight'.

21 On all suspicious sights, sounds and smells, react as the wild animal does and remain perfectly still. If an enemy appears and moves across your front, there is a very good chance that he will not see you. If the enemy appears to be walking towards you, slowly and silently go down on one knee, at the same time bring your weapon into the shoulder aimed at the approaching sound, or carry out Immediate Action drills.

22 Always make positive identification before shooting.

23 If possible, always let the first members of an enemy patrol pass you by, then shoot the third or fourth man. Here again, laid down drills will dictate which member of your patrol will spring the ambush. Remember that in the heat of battle, particularly with today's automatic weapons, the tendency is to fire high, often missing the target altogether. AIM LOW AND SHOOT TO KILL.

24 When operating with an SAS patrol, after the evening meal move on until just before dark, then carry out the 'Basha up' drill (the overnight stop). Always ensure that you are packed and ready to move before first light. Make a final check of the area on first light, then move off to the breakfast halt.

25 When camping, selection of the site will be in such a place that a surprise night attack would be impossible. Use

hammocks for camps on near vertical slopes or crawl into the centre of thick, noise-making vegetation. No lights, no noise, no cooking and all unused equipment to be replaced in bergens.

26 Again when operating as an information gathering patrol, avoid all contact with the enemy. The deeper you get into his secure areas the more relaxed he becomes and so the easier for you to observe and gain intelligence of his movements and activities. Do not leave tracks or signs to tell him that you are in his area. Do not use tracks or trails – loop them.

27 You will be required to make decisions which will influence the lives of other people. Learn quickly to make the correct decision and do not be afraid to express your views. Do not let yourself be talked out of your beliefs.

28 Learn all you can of the enemy in your area. His habits, tactics, customs and practices. Always keep an open mind to new learning – and never become so over-confident that you think that you know it all, as often different areas and enemy personnel will present completely different sets of tactics and drills.

29 Make use of all up-to-date intelligence information and briefings. In particular the 'Going Maps' i.e. tracks, maps, both animal and human, wild fruit trees and vegetable growing areas, the good fishing and game trapping areas, old enemy camp sites, ambush positions, track sitings and known courier routes.

30 It has happened, that an enemy has ambushed and killed twice in the same location using the same tactics. Don't let this happen to you. Read and take note of all 'Contact Reports' and 'Lessons Learned' reports.

The maxim for the modern soldier is:

Once on patrol
Switch on
Stay switched on.
Remember
There is always someone ready
To switch you off
PERMANENTLY!

The next chapter is very closely associated with the military world but because it is such a specialist subject I have set aside a separate chapter for a description of the use of dogs in tracking.

CHAPTER NINETEEN

Dogs and Tracking

This subject has two diametrically opposed facets in the military context. One is the employment of tracker dogs by a tracking team, the other is the study of the techniques of evading a tracker dog and its team.

The employment of tracker dog teams dates back to ancient times but there are still occasions when they are of great benefit to police and also to the military. For instance in the early 'sixties the British Army employed tracker dogs in conjunction with visual trackers to great effect in follow-up operations against the rebels in Brunei.

I will first of all describe how a scent tracker, a dog, can be a great asset to the visual tracker team before going on to describe the evasion techniques which are employed by special forces to combat tracker teams.

SCENT TRACKING – AN ILLUSTRATION

This is a colonial policeman's account of a pursuit and it exemplifies how visual trackers and scent trackers can become a formidable pursuit combination.

After going over fairly easy ground for ten or twelve miles we got into a dry, stony district, where the runaway, knowing he would be tracked, had jumped from rock to rock – a basic deception tactic. The visual tracker was still able to follow the track which consisted of scratch marks on the rocks and small amounts of transferred material.

When we came to a camp of a work party the track was fouled and the visual tracker handed over to the dog handler. The dog ran round the camp and indicated that the fugitive had left in a particular direction.

The visual tracker confirmed that the ground sign was a crude deception – the runaway had changed his boots in the camp and had, at this point been walking backwards – another deception tactic which indicates that the quarry was still aware that he had a pursuit team following him. Very soon it was noticed that the quarry had got tired of wearing strange boots and had started to wear his own again.

After many miles we came to a river, the footprints led straight on into the water. We put the dog across but he didn't find any scent on the far side. He swam back again and found scent of the quarry heading downstream near the river bank. We followed it along the river bank for three miles where the quarry had turned on to a path along which a herd of cattle had recently passed.

The man had obviously nipped in ahead of the herd hoping that they would obliterate his sign, which in fact they did but the dog had no such problem and when the man's route parted company with that of the cattle the dog barely paused – the visual tracker then confirmed the prints as being those of our target and we carried on.

The visual tracker then reported that the sign was very fresh where earth kicked up was damper than the surrounding ground and the edges of the track were sharp, and not rounded over from the sun or wind. We proceeded cautiously and were able to successfully terminate the pursuit.

THE DOG

Despite years of domestication, the dog retains most of the characteristics found in its wild relatives. Primitive man was quick to spot the dog's advantageous traits and to use them to help in hunting and guarding, although there is a recent theory suggesting that about 100,000 years ago the wolf, the forerunner of the domesticated dog, actually adopted man as a means of easy food by scavenging around his leftovers. Either way, modern mankind has adapted the dog's traits to aid in the maintenance of law and order, search and rescue, and to assist the visually and aurally impaired.

Dogs when properly trained and managed can be used to pursue a man efficiently for up to eight hours, depending on terrain and climate, although dogs used in relays can go on much longer than this. Big dogs when fresh can run at speeds between thirty and forty miles an hour over a distance of about a hundred metres, but slow quickly after that. They can maintain a steady eight to ten miles per hour for several hours but, if employed in long pursuits, they are usually limited by the speed of the handler. Thus the average speed is about four miles per hour.

The dog is naturally inquisitive. In many cases its reactions have to be interpreted by a human and herein lies a weakness. The handler may misinterpret or ignore his or her dog's reaction.

From the shape and structure of the dog's eye we have formulated a theory that the dog is short-sighted and sees only in black and white. We know it has difficulty in discerning static objects at a distance of more than fifty metres. However, it has great powers of spotting movement at considerable distances. There is no evidence that a dog's night vision is any better than a human's.

The dog has much more sensitive hearing than a human. It has a greater power of locating the source of a sound and can hear noises of a much higher frequency than those detected by man.

THE SCENT FACULTY

The sense of smell is the faculty in a dog which is vastly superior to a human's. The dog's sense of smell is estimated at about seven to nine hundred times more acute than that of a human. It can detect minute traces of substances or their vapour in the air, on the ground or in contact with objects. Even minor disturbances of the surface of the ground or floor can be sensed by virtue of the alteration of the scent picture around those disturbances.

It is not unreasonable to think in terms of the scent picture for a dog. A dog thinks in smells. It is in another world to a human's. Whatever happens, it seems to appreciate all the odorous characteristics in an environment. We can analyse the scent picture in two basic ways: air scent and ground scent, or we can be more specific and say that it is composed of:

- Objects themselves – animate or inanimate
- Chemicals associated with the objects – deodorants and toiletries on a person, oil on a gun, polish on shoes

- Human smells associated with inanimate objects which have been thrown away or hidden – discardables
- Disturbances of the environment around an object or caused by its passage, such as freshly dug earth, disturbed dust, broken vegetation, smells around hides, vegetation crushed and disturbed by footfalls

THE FACTORS WHICH AFFECT THE SCENT PICTURE

Scent being of a particulate and volatile nature is subject to chemical decay. The first factor adversely affecting the scent picture is therefore the passage of time. The longer the interval between the track being laid and the follow-up the weaker the smell. Other factors, however, accelerate or retard the decay of the scent thus:

- Wind may dissipate scent
- Heavy rain or running water may wash it away
- Strong sunlight will increase evaporation of the scent
- Frozen ground tends to hold scent and release it gradually when it thaws
- A soft warming wind or gentle sunlight will enhance the scent picture by drawing out smells from the environment
- Factors may combine to provide conditions for a good scent picture, for example at night when the warm ground gives off its scent into a cool atmosphere which tends to retain any scent

TRACKER DOGS

These are employed to find the line of the quarry's progress on foot. They work mostly from ground scent but after the passage of time they may follow the evaporating scent given off in the air. Therefore the visual tracker, working in conjunction with a scent tracker, should not be misled by the tracker dog's seemingly erratic progress and the fact that its head is lifted as it moves.

No memory key such as sniffing clothing belonging to the quarry is needed. A handler will experimentally cast a dog around an area until he observes his dog following a particular line. The dog has been trained to follow any distinct track.

SCENT TRAILS

Tracker dogs are taught to follow a certain scent trail. These are strongest in soft going or when the quarry has moved through long grass or vegetation. The scent trail is considerably easier to follow when moving into the wind. The scent trails remain for quite some time, evaporating soonest from hard surfaces within six to eight hours.

MASKING SCENT

There are no guaranteed substances available to stop a tracker dog from following a scent. Successful evasion of dogs depends on the intelligent use of dog evasion techniques and any improvisations that can be utilised to put the tracker dog and his handler off the pursuit.

Some chemicals may destroy scent but if applied they will have characteristic telltale odours of their own. What definitely will not happen is that a smell will be masked by the application of another. Anything added, such as aniseed, just becomes another part of the scent picture to a dog and is a give away of human presence and intent to deceive.

Also if a human covers himself in animal excrement he just smells, to a dog, like a human covered in animal excrement – the key sign is the human smell which is unchanged.

SCENT CHECKS

There are no guaranteed scent checks to throw a tracker dog off a human scent. Three categories of substances are used or have been developed to confuse a dog, they are:

- Attractants: this is meant to resemble the scent of a bitch. The obvious reasoning behind this is that the dog would prefer to follow this rather than the human scent. The down side to the use of this type of substance is that if any should inadvertently get onto the soldier's clothing it will only make the pursuit easier. Also this scent is powerful and the handler will be able to smell it and will realise what has happened – by casting around the handler will be able to continue the track. And of course the tracker dog may be a bitch!
- Repellants: these are primarily designed to put dogs off bitches on heat. They are disagreeable smells but they will

not deter a highly trained dog that is in good working form.

- Decoys: these are designed to be more powerful than the human smell. The idea is for the quarry to drag this for a little distance before discarding it. The hope is that the dog will lose the quarry's scent in the decoy smell and if a well chosen discard point has been made the scent trail will be broken and lost.

PERFORMANCE LEVELS

Dogs are trained to different standards and are temperamentally very different. The normal teaching methods for dogs is the reward system where they are kept hungry and rewarded with food when they find their quarry.

Some dog breeds are particularly suited to this type of work, such as the typical hound breeds and gun dogs, but it must be commented that some are not as enthusiastic as others and I have worked with dogs which have lost interest after only half an hour.

TRACKER DOG TEAMS

Military tracker dog teams normally consist of two or more dogs, plus a visual tracker, snipers and good communications, usually ground to air. Depending on the context of the operation, a tracker team can be placed on to a scent trail very quickly by helicopter and replaced by fresh teams working in relays.

A variation of the employment of dogs in a tracking-related scenario is their use in searches for survivors of earthquakes, avalanches, and during mountain rescue operations. These dogs can be trained to work on or off the lead and either to sit in the area of the casualty when it is located or to return to the handler and sit in front of him as an indication that the dog has located a body.

TRACKER DOG EVASION

This is first and foremost a military skill which a special force's patrol (and in this case I mean a long range raiding or reconnaissance patrol working deep in enemy territory) needs to study if the intelligence indicates the enemy will be deploying tracker dog teams in their search and destroy missions.

EVASION TECHNIQUES

The aim of the evading special forces soldier is to:

- Delay the pursuit
- Break the scent trail

He is taught that the recommended tactics for delaying are:

- Crossing obstacles – it takes twice as long for the dog and handler to cross
- Moving with the wind, not into it – the scent will be blowing away from the pursuit and will be much harder to follow
- Avoid changing direction at obvious places. For example, instead of following a route over a col, turn off before the col and contour around the hillside, or turn off and change direction before a track junction rather than at the junction
- Laying false tracks and backtrack
- Use of streams and hard surfaces such as rocky ground, roads, railway lines, fences, and dry stone walls – the scent will disappear more quickly from these, particularly in sunlight
- Mingling his scent with recent human scent, such as moving down a path or road which has recently been used by locals for a few hundred metres if tactics permit – animal smells or droppings can also assist but are not as effective as human scents

For breaking the scent trail the special forces soldier is taught:

- Gain time in order to allow the scent to become faint due to evaporation
- Use streams to good effect by laying false trails immediately up wind of the entry point, and then by moving downstream and down wind, and then if possible exit onto rocks or any other hard surfaces
- If the situation permits march the last mile or so along hard surfaces or in water
- He should stop and hide up as near first light as possible, thus permitting the day heat to weaken and eventually disperse his scent
- The only known totally effective scent breaking method used by evading troops was to ride on an animal or bicycle

CHAPTER TWENTY

Map-reading

EQUIPMENT

This chapter assumes that the reader is using a Silva, or Silva-type compass. From a tracker's point of view I have found that the best types of map to use for tracking are the different series of the Ordnance Survey. The smallest scale that is of any real use is 1:50 000. Ordnance Survey produce maps with larger scales which contain proportionally more detail. Depending on the area and speed with which you are moving you can decide which is the most appropriate map to use, taking into account the difficulties of handling many large scale maps if you are moving rapidly over an area. Other countries produce similar quality maps if you are working abroad.

THE USES OF MAP-READING TO A TRACKER TEAM

I deliberately left out map-reading as a quality of a tracker in Chapter Five because many of the world's best tracking groups have probably never seen a map, let alone know how to read one. But, having said that it is not a necessity, I still maintain that it is a great adjunct to a tracker's skill set for the following reasons:

- Selection of the quarry's likely route
- Location of your own position
- Prediction of the quarry's actions
- Collating the information and intelligence from other trackers or other pursuits
- Planning pre-emptive operations based on tracking information and intelligence

MAP-READING SUBJECTS AND SKILLS

The following subjects and skills have been selected as being of particular relevance to a tracker. Map-reading and navigation is a huge subject and therefore the following critical selection has been made to provide the student of tracking with what subjects he needs to understand and which skills he must master if he is to track over unfamiliar terrain.

- Conventional symbols and other information contained in the map's margins
- Features of the compass
- Setting the map
- Measuring distances
- Using grid references
- Understanding the different north points
- Converting bearings from grid to magnetic and vice versa
- Taking bearings from the map and assessing your direction of travel
- Plotting position by resection
- Estimating distance covered – speed

CONVENTIONAL SYMBOLS AND OTHER MARGIN INFORMATION
The most important skill in map-reading is to be able to 'read' the map. A good map-reader can look at the map and will immediately start to form a mental picture of what the ground will look like. This takes time and practice but is a skill which can be learnt by all with time and patience. The secret to this technique is the interpretation of the signs and symbols used on the map, and especially the contour lines to visualise the relief of the ground.

Maps are used everywhere in daily life. There are many different types of map. You will have used a road map from a garage, or a map of the Underground, or a street plan of your home town. Each map type is designed for a particular purpose but they all are a two-dimensional representation of the real world. How they convey the information to the reader is via the symbols they use. The key to these symbols is always on the map's margins, along with other essential information such as the scale, and the date of publication. See figure 49 below for examples of legends which show the symbols and their meaning.

FEATURES OF THE COMPASS
The compass itself (see figure 47) is usually mounted at one end of a transparent plastic plate, measuring approximately 12cm by

6 cm, which will have a direction of travel arrow – usually luminous. Incorporated within this base plate you may find a magnifying lens. The short side away from the compass is bevelled. Along the sides of the base plate are various measures, and the short end away from the compass is usually designed as one of a set of romers – see Using Grid References below.

The compass housing rotates and on this rotating bezel are the fixed calibrated compass points. The orienteering or Silva-type compass is either calibrated in degrees or for the military, in mils – this system need not concern the civilian tracker. The bottom of the compass plate is marked with a series of lines running parallel to the north-south calibration and marked with a north arrow. The compass needle, the north half of which is red with a luminous tip, swings freely within this housing.

Figure 47   The Silva compass

SETTING THE MAP

By setting, or orientating, the map we mean holding it in such a way that the details on the map correspond to the features on the ground.

There are two ways to set a map:

The inspection method

This is the easiest way but you must have some idea of where you are on the ground. If you are standing on a straight section of road with a road junction either side of you and sign posts, line up the road on your map with the road you are standing on, making sure the map is pointing in the right direction with reference to the locations indicated on the sign posts. If you are not on a road another linear feature will serve the same purpose. Or you may have to find prominent features on the ground which you can identify on your map, such as a church, bridge, cross-roads, river / stream junction. By identifying features on the ground and on your map you will be able to move your map so that it corresponds to the lie of the land. This is orientating or setting your map by features recognised both on the ground and on the map.

The compass method

This is done by holding the map so that the north of the grid lines of the map are pointing to the north. To effect this one has to take into account the magnetic variation. Using a Silva-type compass, set the magnetic variation on the direction of travel line – see Taking Bearings below and the Different North Points. Then place the compass on the map so that the direction of travel arrow coincides with the north direction of the grid lines. Then rotate the map with the compass laid on top of it until the compass needle coincides with the north pointer of the parallel lines – see figure 48. The map is then set.

MEASURING DISTANCES

It is important that you should be able to estimate and measure distances from your map. If you are moving across country you don't want to miss your objective because you have miscalculated the distance and time it takes to get there.

Scale is the relationship between the size of your map and the area of ground which it depicts. Scale is determined by the number of times the map is smaller than the area of ground which it depicts. The scale shows you the direct relationship in terms of distance between map and ground. By looking at the scale on the map you can tell how many centimetres on the ground are represented by one centimetre on the map. The

Figure 48   Setting a map by the compass method

standard Ordnance Survey map has a scale of 1:50 000. If you walk 50,000 centimetres (500 metres) you will have covered one centimetre on the 1:50 000 scale map.

Check what the scale of your map is and ensure that you know what size the grid squares are – see Using Grid References below. On most maps you will find that the grid squares are one kilometre square, each side being 1000 metres in length. Therefore the distance from corner to corner is for approximate calculations 1.5 kilometres.

Most maps will have a scale bar marked along one edge of the map. The easiest method of measuring a straight line distance is to take a strip of paper and mark the two points, between which you want the distance on the paper, and then read off the distance on the scale bar. To measure the distance along a road or river which winds about simply consider the road to be a number of straight sections. Lay a piece of paper along the first leg and pencil in the start and finish of this leg, then starting at the finish point of the first leg, use this as the start for the second leg and so on until the total distance is marked out along the edge of the piece of paper. Measure this on the scale bar to find the distance on the ground.

USING GRID REFERENCES

A grid is a series of equally spaced parallel numbered lines which are superimposed on the map detail, both vertically and horizontally, to produce a pattern of squares. By the use of this pattern of squares it is possible to give a unique numerical description of a position. This is known as the grid reference. To be absolutely accurate it is an alpha-numeric description because a full grid reference is prefixed by two letters which the Ordnance Survey has allocated to it to distinguish the number from where it will repeat itself elsewhere in the country.

To be able to give and apply grid references it is necessary to understand eastings and northings. The eastings are the vertical lines of the grid system, running north to south on maps and numbered from left to right (east). Northings are the horizontal lines of the grid system running west to east and numbered from the bottom to the top (north).

A four-figure grid refers to one complete grid square. It is defined by the lines which cross at the bottom left-hand corner of the grid square – the south-west corner. In figure 49 the four-figure grid of the square with the X is grid reference 2257. A four-figure grid reference is made up from the two digit eastings, followed by the two digit northings, as in the diagram below. Easting 22 and northing 57 together give the grid reference 2257 which defines the grid square with the cross in it. Use this system when you want to refer to an area contained within a grid square on your map or when there is only one object or feature of the same type within the grid square – for example, the church with a tower in grid square 2257 and the bridge in grid square 2457.

It is essential to remember that when giving or reading a grid reference we always put the eastings first, followed by the northings. There are many ways to remember this such as, 'E'

Figure 49 Sketch illustrating the use of grid references

comes before 'N', or that you go across the map for the eastings and up the map for the northings, therefore, 'You go through the door before you go up the stairs.'

Look again at grid square 2257 with the X in it, you will see that there are two churches, one with a tower and one with a spire. To identify either of these churches you would have to give a further description or, alternatively, you can identify your church by giving a six-figure grid reference.

This refers to one point on the map and it is accurate to within a hundred metres. The grid reference of the church with the tower in grid square 2257 would be 222578 and the bridge in grid square 2457 would be 249573. The two extra numbers in the six-figure grid reference are the third and sixth figures. These extra numbers represent tenths of the grid square. The grid square is divided into tenths, both across and up the square. You then judge how many tenths across and how many tenths up that the feature is. In grid square 2257 look at the location of the church with the tower in the north-west corner. The easting is 22 plus 2 tenths, giving 222, the northing is 57 plus 8 tenths, making 578. This gives a full six-figure grid reference of 222578.

A device called a romer which has a right angle marked in tenths for both the vertical and horizontal axis enables you to give a six figure grid reference at a glance – see figure 50. Simply place the corner of the romer on the feature and read off the third and sixth figure for easting and northings. Silva-type compasses have a built in romer which cuts out the estimation in giving or plotting a six-figure grid reference. Two features of romers need noting. The first is that they are calibrated for specific scales and therefore you have to use the correct one. Secondly, if the point

Figure 50 The use of a romer

falls between two marks always take the lower number not the nearest number, this is because the grid reference as pointed out with a four figure grid reference refers to the south-west corner of the particular square which you are describing.

Remember, with a six-figure grid reference first give all three figures across, the eastings, before you give the northings.

THE DIFFERENT NORTH POINTS

There are three norths indicated on Ordnance Survey maps. They are:

- True North
- Magnetic North
- Grid North

True North is the direction of the North Pole and is shown by the lines of longitude on a map or chart.

Magnetic North is the direction in which a freely suspended compass needle points and because of the physical character-istics of the earth it varies annually and by different amounts in different regions. All this information will be written in the margins of the large scale maps which you use as a tracker.

Grid North is the direction of the grid lines on the map. This is different to True North because the grid lines on a flat map cannot geometrically fit identically to the lines of latitude and longitude of the curved surface of the earth.

CONVERTING BEARINGS

The bearing which you take off a map is a grid bearing, whereas the one which is shown by your compass is a magnetic bearing. Therefore you need a system to be able to convert from one to the other.

The method is to check the information on the map about the magnetic variation (whether it is east or west of grid north), its annual rate of change for the area, and the date of publication of the map. From these facts you can work out the magnetic variation today.

A way to remember which way the conversion goes from magnetic to grid bearings is:

From Mag to Grid Get Rid
From Grid to Mag Add

Note: This rhyme only applies if Magnetic North is to the east of Grid North, otherwise the rule is reversed. But for the most part in Britain the rhyme applies.

TAKING BEARINGS FROM THE MAP AND ASSESSING YOUR DIRECTION OF TRAVEL

Using an orienteering-type compass, line up the edge of the compass base plate on the objects between which you want the bearing. Ensure that the direction of travel arrow is pointing in the appropriate direction, that is normally, from where you are to where you want to go – see figure 51. Rotate the compass housing until the parallel lines in the base of the housing are parallel with and, in the same direction as, the north-south grid lines of the map.

This is the grid bearing between the two points. Before you can use the compass to assess your direction of travel you have to adjust this for the magnetic variation – see above.

Figure 51 Taking a bearing from a map

When you have rotated the compass housing so that the reading against the direction of travel arrow takes into account the magnetic variation, usually by adding several degrees in Britain, you now have the magnetic bearing set on your compass.

Your intended direction of travel is found by holding the compass horizontal (so that the compass needle is free to swing) and by moving it around until the north of the compass needle is superimposed over the north pointer of the parallel lines in the base of the compass housing.

PLOTTING POSITION BY RESECTION

If you are unsure of your position you can plot it accurately on the map by using resection. Basically all you have to do is to locate two objects or features on the ground which you can identify on the map, take bearings visually to them from where you are, convert these magnetic bearings to grid bearings, plot the two bearings on the map, and where the lines cross is your position.

To find a bearing from you to a feature simply point the direction of travel arrow at the object and then, holding the compass horizontally, rotate the compass housing until the north pointer on the housing base is under the compass needle. Remember this is a magnetic bearing and needs converting before putting on the map.

ESTIMATING DISTANCE COVERED – SPEED

As well as being able to use the above mentioned skills you should take time to consider how far you are able to move in different types of country and weather conditions. You can estimate this by knowing what your average pace is for the various conditions. For example, walking on a flat road you may cover 4 miles per hour. Therefore if you have been walking for 45 minutes you will have covered 3 miles. Another way is to count your paces – pacing. If you know how many paces you take to cover 100 metres, then it is quite easy to work out the distance you have covered. The best way to do this is to measure your pace over a known 100 metres distance counting every time your right foot touches the ground. Do this walking, then again running, and note the difference. You will find a difference going up or down hill and in different terrain and weather conditions. As a basic guide I average about 64 paces per 100 metres walking and 40 to 45 when running. In the time it takes to walk 200 metres on the flat you could climb a 25 metre slope, cover 150 metres through primary forest or travel 50 metres through thick undergrowth. With experience you will be able to make a good informed estimate of the distance you have travelled.

As I mentioned earlier, map-reading can never be considered a prerequisite for tracking, but if you are intending tracking any-where other than your own area it is an important skill. Not only does it make the relaying of information easier, but it adds interest and can be essential for safety in the remoter areas.

CHAPTER TWENTY-ONE

Human Prints

A breakdown description of a bare footprint will enable a tracker to describe fully what he has seen without omitting any detail – he will be able to extract from the print the maximum amount of information. We then move on logically to a full description of how a tracker studies a print made by a quarry wearing foot-wear. The next stage is to analyse the walking action to see how a track, that is a series of prints, is produced. And the chapter concludes with sections on what can be deduced from these detailed observations by noting what causes peculiarities in a print or a track.

BARE FOOTPRINTS

To find some reference point the footprint is divided as in figure 52. There is a fixed axis and a line at right angles to this. The axis of the foot is a line that passes through the centre of the heel to the centre of the big toe. From this axis the other reference line is that which just touches the lowest edge of the little toe. As a further help a third line has been drawn from the tip of the big toe to the tip of the little toe.

The analysis follows the scheme below:

- The toes – count them, there are not always five
- The pad under the toe – this is the only part of the toe that normally comes into contact with the ground when walking
- The length of the toes – long or short
- The relative length of the toes – in some cases the second toe is longer than the big toe
- The position of the toes with reference to the diagonal line – in some cases the third toe is furthest from the diagonal line, in other cases the fourth
- Spacing – in some cases there is a space between the

AXIS

Figure 52   Human footprint

second and third toes, in others there is a larger space
between the third and fourth
- The configuration of the forward edge of the impression of
  the sole and the toe prints
- The shape of the outer edges of the print
- The form of the instep – pronounced or weak
- The size and shape of the heel
- The size and shape of the ball of the foot
- The pattern of the area connecting the heel and ball pads
- Any peculiarities – creases, cracks, and scars

When we consider these features of the human footprint and the
differences that can exist it is easy to comprehend the possibility

of a trained tracker being able to recognise one person from another by their footprints.

The tracker confronted with a foot and a footprint made by the foot has to realise that they will not necessarily be one and the same in form because of the weight distribution, the gait of the quarry, and the ground irregularities. Also if the quarry is attempting to confuse a tracker he may change his gait which can alter the appearance of his footprints. For instance, a shuffle, or placing the foot at a different angle, or a slight twist as the foot meets the ground will make all the difference to the impression made.

FOOTWEAR PRINTS

The footwear print is a result of the footwear itself (that is how it left the factory or the cobbler's last), how it has been worn since then (duration of wear and characteristics of the wearer), and how it was placed on the tracking medium by the quarry.

In setting out to study a footwear mark the following points should be noted:

- Length of footwear mark from heel to toe
- Breadth of sole at its broadest point
- Length of the heel from the front edge behind the instep to the back of the heel
- Breadth of the heel
- Height of heel – if on soft soil
- Number, shape and position of nails, if any
- Any distinctive marks made by the sole or heel
- Any logos or writing
- Wear marks
- The shape of the various parts of the print – the toe, heel, and sole
- Any indication as to the composition of the footwear – rubber, leather, rope, canvas, plastic
- If there is a succession of footmarks, length of stride from the toe of one footmark to the back of the heel of the next successive footmark
- Any indications of sex or age from such features as size or footwear style

When trying to match a print to a particular piece of footwear be careful not to make the obvious mistake of fitting the specimen footwear over the original sign and thus fouling or obliterating it.

As with all important pieces of sign it is well worth recording the details either by sketching them or photographing them. Always leave a scale marker alongside the print for future reference purposes.

PRINTS AND THE WALKING ACTION

To gain a full insight into what we are looking at when we study a human footprint it is necessary to have an understanding of the walking action. A slow-motion picture shows you the movements which a man makes in walking. This type of demonstration is useful to illustrate the walking action and how it influences the sign. The muscular motions which propel a man forward have their counterpart in the track that he leaves on the ground.

The following is a description of the walking action. From the standing position a man leans forward. This throws his centre of gravity in the direction in which he intends to go. As he does this he commences to bend the knee of the leg he intends to move forward first. We will assume that he intends to step off with the left leg. He bends the left knee and at practically the same time, in order to relieve the ankle, he raises the left heel from the ground. As the leg moves forward the whole of the sole of the foot leaves the ground, the toe being the last to lose contact. At the same time he leans slightly over to the right throwing his weight gradually on to the right leg and foot until they bear the full weight of his body. The right foot is flat on the ground and the weight of the body distributed equally along the length of the sole from heel to toe until he bears the full weight of his body. The left leg is advanced and simultaneously the centre of gravity is thrown further forward when there is a danger of the balance being lost the left leg straightens out and the left heel touches the ground.

In the meantime the right leg is bent at the knee and the right heel is forced to leave the ground, with the result that the weight of the body is borne on the back of the left heel and the front of the right toe, the centre of gravity of the body being swung forward and to the left by the push of the right toe. The direction of this force causes the man to strike the ground with the outer side of the back of the heel which goes downwards and forwards into the ground, pushing the soil, if soft, in front of it. This soil is gradually forced down and forward as the left foot comes to the ground from heel to toe. Before the right toe leaves the ground it gives a final push towards the left foot which has the effect of pushing the soil away in a contrary direction.

All the weight is then borne on the left foot and the right swings forward, causing the centre of gravity again to change direction towards the right. The effect of this change of direction is to cause the left foot to exert pressure similarly. When the heel touched the ground it pushed the soil forward and slightly outwards, then it pressed it straight down as the pressure passed directly above it and now it presses it to the rear and outwards as the left heel begins to lift for its second step. This roll of the foot is what makes the impression of the foot broader than the foot itself actually is.

Studying this movement tells us where to look for the most marked impressions of the foot on the ground. The two most marked are those made by the outer side of the back of the heel and the inner side of the toe. The next two are those made by the ball of the foot behind the big toe and by the outer side of the foot behind the little toe. Then there is a small heap of soil thrown forward by the back of the heel and pressed down by the flat of the heel and finally a certain amount of soil thrown back by the toe and not pressed down.

Two important points arise. On hard ground there may be no other mark left on the ground except where the heel first struck the ground and where the toe last left it. The faster a person walks the more soil will be dispatched by the toe and that soil will be loose.

It will be noticed that in the ordinary walk the heel meets the ground first and the toes point slightly outward, following the direction of the thrust made by the opposite foot. I have emphasised 'ordinary' because if the person is thinking about how he walks he can alter this profile (see Prints and Deductions below).

We now have the ordinary marks left by an average man at an ordinary walk. The relationship of the left footmark to the right will vary according to the man. The distance between each footmark will be slightly over thirty inches. If a string were taken

Figure 53 The walking action of man

and stretched along the centre of the line of walk, it would pass over both heels, but the left toes would fall to the left of it, and the right toes to the right.

SPEED

If the walk is slower, more balance will be required; it is just the same on one's feet as on a bicycle, and so the heels will lie more off the centre line to the left and right respectively. The slower the walk the more there will be a tendency to place them wider apart, and the toes at a greater angle – figure 54/1.

When a man trots, figure 54/2, he merely speeds up his walk and the track he leaves is speeded up accordingly. The same characteristics in regard to the parts of the print most marked and the soil pressed forward or back will be present but to a marked degree. The distance between each step will be lengthened and, as he has more balance because he is going faster, there will be a tendency for the marks to be in a straighter line. It is to be noticed that the impression of the toes will be deeper and that of the heels correspondingly lighter, but in soft soil the marks of the heels will be easily apparent.

Figure 54   Tracks of the same quarry under different conditions

GRADIENT

In walking up a slope the heel strikes less and less deeply as the hill gets steeper because when the foot is brought to the ground the leg is bent at the knee. There is also a tendency to walk with the toes pointing straighter forward. In walking down a slope at an ordinary pace the feet are kept practically straight but more flat to the ground so that the toe and the back of the heel strike less deeply than when walking on the level. In hurrying down a slope, however, the heels are stuck sharply into the ground to act as brakes and the paces are considerably longer.

TRAINING OR PANIC FLIGHT

A significant difference can be seen in the track of a man trained to run fast against an untrained runner. A trained runner sprinting will bring the ball of his foot only to the ground and thrust off with his toes. He leaves no marks of his heels. His paces are much longer than at a trot and the marks left by his toes are in a straight line with very marked backwards facing push marks – figure 54/3.

An untrained man running fast will probably show a different kind of track altogether. It is quite possible that he will bring his heel down to the ground first in the same way as in walking only with increased force. His feet tend to point out again, as in walking, and the line of his track will not be so straight. The untrained man running fast is manifesting a phenomenon known as 'panic flight', to which even a trained runner is prone in times of danger.

I have personal experience of 'panic flight'. One summer's day as a young boy I was accompanying my father on a fishing expedition. On our way to the river we had to cross a few meadows. We were climbing out of a dip and coming over a low crest when we were surprised by a bull. We just managed to make our exit from the field ahead of the snorting animal.

We may call the walk, the trot and the sprint the three main gaits which the human animal adopts, but for the purposes of the classification of human tracks I propose to add four more:
- those made by a man walking backwards
- those made by a man who is carrying a weight

- those made by a man who is exhausted
- and those made by men suffering from some physical infirmity

WALKING BACKWARDS

The movements and the sign left by a man walking ordinarily have been fully described and it stands to reason that if he is going to reverse the direction of these movements that the effects of them on the ground will also be reversed. This is, of course, precisely what happens, thus:

- Instead of pushing off from his toe at each step he pushes off from his heel
- Instead of his heel first striking the ground at the completion of each step, his toe does
- The mark he makes on the ground shows then a push back from the heel
- There is no push back from the toe
- The steps are shorter
- The line of walk is uncertain
- The toes may turn in
- There may be a shuffle of the soil in a backward direction from toe to heel

CARRYING A LOAD

If a man is carrying a burden he has to propel himself forward and, in addition, he has to force the extra weight forward – see figure 54/4. So we get these characteristics showing in the track:

- The steps are shorter
- The feet are planted wider apart laterally
- The line of march is uncertain as the extra weight affects the balance
- The indentations are deeper than they would ordinarily be, especially at the toe

There is the obvious dilemma as to whether the quarry is heavy or whether the quarry is light and is carrying a pack. The uncertainty of the line is the strongest clue to differentiate and, of course, there may be corroborating evidence such as pack marks at resting places or against trees.

EXHAUSTED

If a man is exhausted he loses some control over his legs. Anyone who has run a gruelling race realises this fact to the full. Those who haven't have probably seen such a race and have noticed how the runners stagger off the track. This isn't histrionics for the camera. The track gives a true picture of the extent of the exhaustion. The marks left on the ground show that:

- The feet have strayed from a central well-balanced line
- The feet are inclined to cross over each other
- The line of advance is very uncertain
- The outer edges of each impression are deeply indented
- There is no cleanness or definite pattern in the track as a whole – it shambles about

A similar track would be left by: a wounded man but there may be other evidence such as blood stains or medical discardables; or a drunken man in which case there may be discardables such as bottles or there may be vomit or many urination sites.

OTHER DEDUCTIONS FROM PRINTS

This material should be cross-referenced with Chapter Fifteen to give a full description of the intelligence which can be gleaned from prints by the trained tracker. It cannot be over-emphasised how important it is for the tracker to sketch the first good print he finds of his quarry. The sketch will be an invaluable record later on in the pursuit to which he will be able to refer. The following gives a detailed analysis:

- An estimate of height can be deduced from the length of the stride and from the length of the footmark
- Weight can be deduced from the depth of the impression – it has already been noted that this can be affected by the load the quarry is carrying
- The combination of the height and weight will give an indication as to build but further characteristics are seen in the case of obese persons in that they are inclined to plant their feet farther apart to afford them more balance and are also inclined to turn their toes outwards
- The socio-economic group by the type and upkeep of the footwear

Physical condition of the quarry

This has a considerable effect on a track:

- Knock-kneedness shows up with the heels apart, the right heel falls a little to the right and the left heel a little to the left of the central line of the track. The inner side of the back of his heel, and not the outer side, will strike the ground first and leave a correspondingly marked impression
- A wound, injury or malformation of the leg will frequently entail a difference in the length of stride
- Lameness is indicated by two footmarks close together followed by a space and another two prints – usually the short pace is made by the sound leg as this is bearing the weight a disproportionate amount of the time thus allowing the lame leg to be thrown forward further
- A damaged heel's impression will be light, as with a sore toe
- If the leg is stiff, the steps may be of equal length, but there may be signs of the foot brushing into place on the ground, usually from an outward and backward direction
- A blind person leaves a short pace, the line of march is apt to be uncertain, the feet are planted wider apart, there may be marks of a stick or a dog
- Age influences the walk to a considerable degree in that old people are apt to become infirm, their powers of balance are lessened, entailing a spreading out of the feet, the line of march is not so straight, and the steps are shorter, and sometimes a shuffling action can be detected

CHAPTER TWENTY-TWO

Animal Prints

For anyone who has an interest in wildlife, this chapter gives the background information essential to a fuller development of the associated tracking skills. From a brief study of the anatomical differences we progress to a description of the different methods of locomotion and how this affects the subject's sign. The sign of some of the more common mammals found in temperate areas are then described before the chapter concludes with an account indicating the main variations in the sign of the major bird groupings.

The reader who lives in or is intending to visit a tropical or sub-tropical area is encouraged to read one of the specialist area-focused texts such as *Signs of the Wild* by Clive Walker for Southern Africa.

Figure 55 gives a few examples of some of the spoor likely to be encountered on a safari.

ANATOMICAL CLASSIFICATIONS
The formation of the foot has changed over time so that today we have three marked divisions under which the feet of animals can be classified.

Animals that walk on the flat of the foot are termed sole-walkers or plantigrades. The sole-walkers, as a class, are the most widespread. We ourselves are sole-walkers and have as our companions such diverse animals as bears, porcupines, hedgehogs, monkeys, gorillas, badgers, otters, hares and rabbits.

There are those that walk on their toes, toe-walkers, or digitigrades. This class includes all the members of both the canine and the feline genus.

The third group are those which walk on the points of their toes, like ballet dancers. In the process of time their toes, or four of them at least, have grown together until they have become

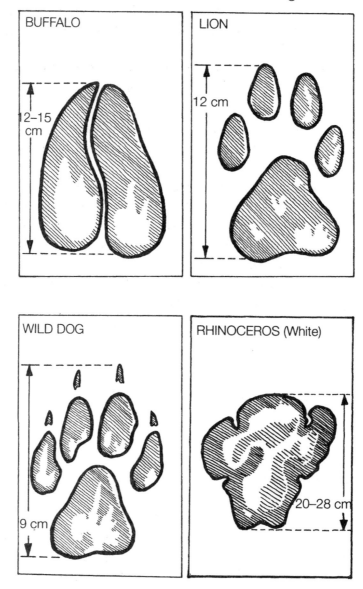

Figure 55   Four African mammals

hooves. This class is known as the nail-walkers or ungulates and can be subdivided into two – animals with a solid hoof, and animals with a cloven hoof. Examples of this class are: horses, mules, zebras, cows, deer, sheep and goat.

For tracking purposes we are then interested in another classification of animals and that is dependent upon the structure of their limbs.

The first class comprises those animals whose legs are about of equal length. In this large class are included horses, cattle, pigs, deer, canines and felines.

The second class contains animals whose hind legs are much longer than their front legs, such as hares, rabbits, squirrels and kangaroos.

To the third class belong those animals whose legs are short in proportion to their bodies, such as otters, weasels, stoats, ferrets, mink and martens.

The fourth class includes those animals whose legs are very short in proportion to their bodies, and whose bodies are also very large such as badgers, hedgehogs and porcupines.

It is not so easy to classify every animal accurately in one only of the above classes according to the way it moves but the groupings are a useful aid to the wildlife tracker. Some animals will show characteristics of gait which appear to belong to two classes, sometimes walking and sometimes hopping, for instance the squirrel.

METHOD OF LOCOMOTION AND HOW IT AFFECTS SIGN

The normal walk is the basis of all tracking comparison whether with human beings or other animals, just as we considered the gait of humans in the previous chapter, so we have to study the various methods of locomotion so as to be in a better position to analyse the sign left by the non-human quarry.

FIRST CATEGORY – EQUAL LENGTH LIMBS

As with the study of the walk of man, watching a video or a slow-motion film will highlight the order and way in which an animal lifts and places his legs. When a horse walks it plants its feet diagonally – see figure 56. If the near (right) fore foot touches the ground first, the off (left) hind foot is placed next, then the off-fore foot, and lastly the near-hind foot. Thus it moves all four feet one after another, so that four footfalls may be heard, but it does not move the two on the same side one after the other.

The tracks shown in figure 59/5 show the distinctive side by side position of the prints. All the animals in this class move in this way, except the camel. The camel does not move diagonally but lifts its feet in the following rotation: near-fore, near-hind,

The Walk

Figure 56 The walking action of a horse

The Trot

Figure 57 The trot

off-fore, off-hind. It is this method of progression that sets up a swaying movement from side to side that proves very inconvenient and sometimes disastrous to the novice rider.

The track left by the horse at a walk differs according to the individual. Where the hind registers in relationship to the fore is a significant recognition feature, that is, whether it is behind, superimposed on, or in front of the mark made by the fore hoof. In a very heavy horse, such as a cart-horse, the hind hoof will show behind the fore hoof, whereas in a light riding horse the hind hoof will be in front of the fore hoof. The relative positions of these marks also depends on the speed.

The trot, figure 57, is merely a hastened walk, and the gait is just the same but quicker. The feet touch the ground in the same rotation, but as two feet touch the ground almost at the same time only the noise of two footfalls will be heard. The track itself appears more in a straight line because the animal has more balance in consequence of the speed, and plants its feet more under the centre of its body. The mark of the hind foot will almost invariably show in front of the mark of the fore foot, and the distance between paces will obviously be greater.

The gallop is a series of leaps, as figure 58 shows. The hind legs serve mainly to propel the animal forward and the fore legs to balance or brace the body. For this reason the hind legs are planted more or less side by side, while the fore legs are planted apart from, and one behind the other. The resultant track is like a magnified rabbit's track, for, owing to the speed at which the animal is moving, the hind hoofs hit the ground well in front of the fore hoofs.

SECOND CATEGORY – UNEQUAL LENGTH LIMBS
Animals whose hind legs are longer than their fore legs progress by a kind of leapfrog movement – see figure 59/4. The hind feet come round the fore legs and are thrown ahead of the fore feet. In this class of animals the hind feet are longer than the fore feet and can be easily distinguished.

THIRD CATEGORY – SHORT LEGS/LONG BODY
The jump made by members of this group is a curious loping snakelike movement – see figure 59/1 and 59/2. The movement is rather like that of a porpoise in the water – a series of curves.

The Gallop

Figure 58   The gallop

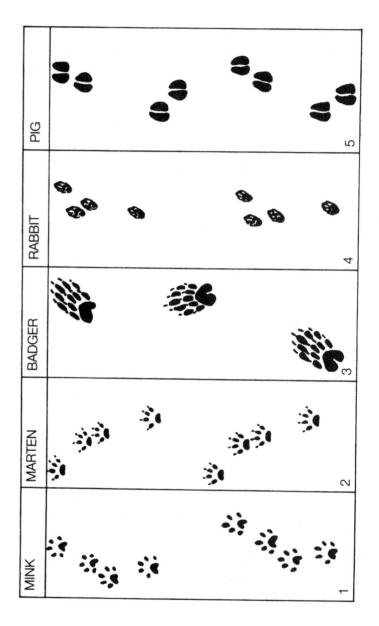

Figure 59 Tracks of four different animal categories

The two fore feet leave the ground and come down together side by side, the animal's body doubles up like a drawn bow, and the hind feet follow, landing almost directly on the same spot, while the fore feet go off on the next bound, so that the trail shows apparently one pair of tracks side by side at regular intervals. Occasionally some of the animals in this class will make short bounds with all four feet at the same time. At a faster pace the hind feet may seemingly outstrip the fore feet and land in front of them.

FOURTH CATEGORY — SHORT LEGS/LARGE BODY
The animals of the fourth class, figure 59/3, usually walk turning their hind feet in to a marked degree and spreading all four feet out wide apart laterally. As a general rule the hind foot registers over the mark of the fore foot and across it, heels out, toes in. Occasionally, when alarmed, they will leap but because of their bulk, the distance between successive tracks is short.

These classifications, foot and gait, have been adopted so as, by a process of elimination, to narrow down the possibilities of the identity of any one track that is noticed. They are an aid and help to throw light on the characteristics and habits of the quarry.

DISTINGUISHING MARKS
Animals, like human beings, leave sign specific to the individual. Just as we noted in the previous chapter with a human quarry, it is a matter of observant, concentrated, systematic study of the print that allows the tracker to distinguish his quarry from that of another member of the same species.

Even with a solid-hoofed animal it is possible to distinguish the print of one from another – likewise if the horse is shod there are differences in the shoe.

Also, when we study the track as a whole, there are differences in the length of stride and the position in which the feet are placed in relation to each other.

In the case of cloven-hoofed animals the splitting of the hoof, and the shape of the two halves of the hoof are also points which will help the tracker to identify the spoor of his quarry. The split in the hoof in most cloven-hoofed animals varies according to age and sex, apart from any accidents that the animal in question has experienced. The male usually has a squarer toe. The two halves of the foot are not uniform in shape and size, and the difference between the two is an important clue in identifying individuals.

DOMESTICATED ANIMALS

Cattle, sheep and pigs leave their prints in two parallel lines, one on each side of the central line of the track. The impression of all four feet are clearly seen. In cattle there is a general tendency for the hoof to open out more at the toe than the heel in full grown animals. The sheep has a smallish, pointed hoof, whilst the pig, on soft ground, shows the marks of the dew claws behind the marks of the hooves. Goats usually place their hind feet well in front of the fore and have a more irregular cleft.

The following illustrations, figure 60, show some of the more common animal prints and tracks which have a worldwide distribution and a few of the larger species. These examples will help the student to start to differentiate between species and then between individuals within that species.

DEER

In most kinds of deer the tracks register, that is the marks of the fore feet are covered by the marks of the hind. A deer track will

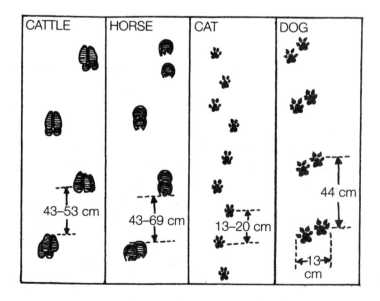

Figure 60   Prints of animals with a worldwide distribution

show the condition of the animal to a great extent. The doe nearly always registers and when heavy in young the feet will be spread wider apart laterally. The buck varies according to the season. When full of strength in the early spring its hind feet will overstep the marks made by the fore feet. As the rutting season progresses they will drop back and register, and when he is worn out and out of condition it will be found that the hind feet lag behind the fore feet.

FOX

A fox leaves a pad-mark rather like that of a small dog but there are several points of dissimilarity. The impression is narrower by comparison with its length. The hind pad is smaller compared with the size of the toes. And a careful examination of a clear print will show traces of hair between the toes and the pad leaving a furry margin, as opposed to the more clear-cut impression of the dog's paw.

The fox's track seems to be more akin to that of the cat than the dog. The dog splashes along and seems to take special delight in putting its feet in muddy places, whilst the fox walks deliberately and avoids wet and dirty places and behaves in this respect like a cat. Usually, the fox registers its hind paw over the impression made by the fore paw, again as the cat does.

CATS AND DOGS

The toe-walkers comprise the two great tribes of canines and felines, and a comparison of the track of the dog with that of the cat brings out an extraordinary number of differences. These are entirely due to the characteristics of the two different types of animals and these characteristics arise out of their mode of life.

The dog leaves a zigzag track, like a horse, with the marks of all four feet showing in two parallel lines. The marks of the nails can be seen. The cat leaves a comparatively straight track which shows only one line of marks more or less on a central line.

The cat, as its wild cousins the leopard and the tiger do to this day, lived amongst the jungle and stalked its prey by stealth. Speed was not so much a consideration as quietness. It stalked carefully along, planting its hind feet in exactly the same spot where its fore feet had been, so that only the marks of the hind paws were left on the ground. This was important, because if the hind paw snapped a twig the noise might alarm its prey. As a stalker it is a past master and can balance in any positions.

Note: There is one interesting point in connection with the toe-walkers that might be mentioned, and that is that the back of the fore foot is concave and the back of the hind foot convex, just as the back of the palms of our hand is concave and the back of our heel is convex.

RABBITS AND HARES

The best way to distinguish between the various types of animal whose hind legs are longer than their fore legs is by the size of the actual track and the distance between the successive marks. For instance, it might be easy to distinguish the print of a kangaroo from that of a hare but not so easy to distinguish the print of a hare from a rabbit. But with the whole track there should be no such problem, especially if the tracker takes into account all the evidence including the locality.

In these leapfrog tracks, an important point to be certain of is the direction in which the animal is travelling. At first it is difficult to grasp that a four-footed animal's hind legs can come in front of the fore legs.

RATS

The third class of the animals with short legs and long bodies again show peculiar characteristics between the various types, although most of them are also sole-walkers. These characteristics depend more upon the length of the bound than upon the size of the individual marks. Many will show the marks of the tail as a drag between the two parallel lines of the track. Rats seem to leave their tails behind them more than mice do but the different varieties of each leave a slightly different track. A water vole and a common brown rat may be difficult to distinguish from each other by the track they leave but in this case the environment should be taken into account.

OTTERS

The tail marks the otter, coupled with his size, and the fact that he walks the occasional few steps.

BADGERS

Amongst the short legged/large bodied category of animals, the badger will register the hind foot across the fore.

BIRDS

Because of the great similarity between the tracks of many birds it is important for the naturalist using tracking skills to realise that locality is the most important point to be considered.

The main differences are between birds that perch in trees, birds that walk on the ground and birds that live on the water. The tree-percher, the sparrow, chaffinch and thrush, generally hop along the ground with both feet together and in line with each other. The ground-walkers, such as pheasant and grouse, walk along somewhat like we do, first one foot then the other. The water birds, duck, goose and swan, all waddle along with their toes turned in.

Perchers

Amongst the tree-perchers, see figure 61/1, it is possible to identify one kind from another only by the size and now and then by the tail and wing marks. For instance, the chaffinch leaves a small mark, with sometimes the flick of the tail showing on the ground, whereas the sparrow's track shows larger marks, and the thrush even larger ones with greater distances between them.

Walkers

The ground-walkers, figure 61/2, are mostly game birds and it will be found that the toes of game birds are set much wider apart than those of, say, rooks and blackbirds. The angle of the outside toes of game birds are set at, or greater than, a right angle, whereas the angle formed by the outside toes of other birds is less than ninety degrees. Again it will be noticed that the toes of the game bird are of even thickness almost to the tips, whilst the toes of others taper. Pheasants and partridges especially have peculiarly smooth toes which leave a clean cut impression, whilst such birds as pigeons have coarser scales which leave a far rougher mark. The pheasant's track, however,

Figure 61 Tracks left by different categories of birds

is larger than that of the partridge and its middle toe stands almost in a straight line with its tail. The cock pheasant trails his tail behind him. The snipe makes neat tracks which might be mistaken for the tracks of other birds if it were not for the little round holes here and there which show where it has probed for food. The woodcock's tracks are similar but larger and again beak marks are found.

Water birds

The tracks of water birds are usually so much alike that again only the difference in size makes it possible to distinguish between the species. Their webbed feet clearly distinguish them from the ground-walkers and tree-perchers – figure 61/3.

Waders

The feet of the waders may show slight webbing but more usually it will be found that the toes are long and stand well out from each other so as to give a greater surface on which the birds can walk in the mud – figure 61/4.

CONCLUSION

The trained keeper in pursuit of game birds usually pays more attention to other signs than the tracks he may be able to see on the ground. Feathers will be found in places where birds have taken sand-baths, small paths leading here and there in the grass will show where birds have eaten. The place where a bird has been feeding, as well as the food itself, will give a clue to its identity.

Undoubtedly, snow is the most suitable medium for bird tracks. Snow not only shows the marks made by the feet of birds but the marks of their wings and tails as well. For instance, when a magpie alights on snow it will leave a clear impression of its tail-feathers as well as of its outspread wing-feathers – see below.

Figure 62 Sign left by birds taking off from snow-covered ground

CHAPTER TWENTY-THREE

Vehicle Sign

You may recall that the definition of sign given in Chapter Two was 'any physical indication which is left on the environment by the passage of any animal or inanimate object'. No account of tracking can be complete without considering the study of the sign left by vehicles

The traffic police and insurance assessors have built up a mass of forensic information relating to speed, direction and roadworthiness which they can extract from vehicle marks left at the scene of a traffic accident. I do not intend trespassing on this specialist area because this book's raison d'être is tracking which, by definition, is following the line of the sign.

TYRE TRACKS

Just as a tracker studying the print of an animal or a human has a check list of features, so he has when recording the details of a vehicle print. The following are the details in which the tracker is interested:

- Depth of tread
- Depth of impression
- Distinguishing features of the tread – wear pattern
- Pattern of the tyre
- Width of the tyre tread – weight of the vehicle and its load, the pressure of the tyre
- Variations of the different wheels
- Width of track will indicate the type of vehicle
- Direction of travel:
    - indicated by the tread pattern
    - stones are pushed forward slightly and then kicked back
    - passing over a bump, the tyres will broaden out momentarily as they impact on landing

- small areas of dust, mud and water will be thrown out and slightly backwards
- puddles of water, if driven through fast, will push the water forward
- reversing – uncertain line

Just as in other tracking scenarios the tracker is trying to gain as much information from the sign as possible, so it is with vehicle sign. And to this end the emotional state of the driver can be estimated to a degree by the presence of skid marks where the vehicle has been drawn to a halt or where it has sped off.

Figure 63   Typical tread pattern left by a car tyre

VEHICLE LOADS

Often the load of a vehicle, especially a goods vehicle, can leave a great deal of useful information for the tracker which will link a vehicle to two sites and a particular route.

The deposits can be left on the road/ground in the form of drips from a bulk liquid carrier or in overhanging vegetation from other types of load.

BICYCLES

Two-wheel vehicles have an inherent advantage for the tracker in that as they move more slowly the rider has greater difficulty maintaining his balance. The physical state of the rider and/or the direction of travel of a bicycle can be judged by the track, in that the straighter it is the faster it is moving so a tired rider (or one who is riding uphill) will leave a front wheel track which swings left and right of the axis.

TRACKING COMBINED VEHICLE/FOOT JOURNEYS

As was mentioned in Chapter Nineteen, there is only one guaranteed method of thwarting a scent tracker and that is by riding on an animal or a bike. But the tracker who is aware of the significance of vehicle prints and has studied them will be able to link in with the scent tracker and frustrate this ploy by linking the vehicle prints at one entry/exit point with those at another.

The two entry/exit sites may not only be linked by vehicle and footprint impression but by transfer of material from one site to the other where it is totally foreign.

ANIMAL-DRAWN VEHICLES

The fact that you as a tracker have identified the quarry as an animal-drawn vehicle is in itself very useful distinguishing information. You then have the advantage of being able to draw conclusions from two sources – the prints of the animal and those of the vehicle.

CHAPTER TWENTY-FOUR

Preserving Prints

For the tracking instructor, or the naturalist who is studying a species, it is often a requirement to be able to preserve a specimen of a print. In this chapter I will outline the usual method.

There are also recent developments which can be used to preserve the information from a print – I refer the reader to Chapter Twenty-Five and the section on digital photography.

Plaster of Paris is widely available from art shops as well as the usual suppliers, such as chemists and builders' merchants. The best plaster is that used by dentists – fine Italian plaster. In any case care must be taken to see that the plaster is absolutely fresh and that it is kept in an airtight tin as exposure to the air will render it stale so that it will not set readily when mixed with water.

THE TECHNIQUE (Figure 64)
When a track has been found carefully remove any loose material, whether vegetation or debris, that may be lying across it but take great care not to mark the print itself. Forceps or a photographer's blower brush are useful at this stage – Figure 64/1.

If the track is shallow or on sloping ground it will be necessary first of all to build a wall or bund around the mark with twigs or mud or even strips of cardboard so as to keep the plaster on the track whilst it is in a liquid form.

Pour some water into a container and sift the plaster into it, breaking up any lumps as much as possible – Figure 63/2. Stir all the time and keep on adding plaster or water until the mixture is the consistency of thick cream and can just be poured out of the container. The quantity of the mixture required will naturally vary with the size of the print but it is better to make too much than too little. Tap the container on the ground or with a knife so as to get rid of air bubbles.

Pour the mixture gently into the crevices of the print – Figure 63/3 – and to the sides of the print, taking care to avoid air bubbles. Be sure that the cast is made sufficiently thick by adding successive layers of the mixture, as otherwise it will break in transit.

Drying time for the cast will vary according to atmospheric conditions and the dampness of the ground itself. A pinch of salt

Figure 64   Making a plaster cast of a print

added to the mixture usually has the effect of making the cast dry more quickly and of rendering its composition stronger. Monitor drying by gentle finger pressure. It usually takes between fifteen and thirty minutes to set, depending on how much water was mixed with the plaster – Figure 63/4.

When the cast is nearly dry scratch on the back of it the place, date, your name and the name of the quarry or some identification. At the same time make a record in your note book of all details in connection with the print – type of ground, weather conditions, age of track, quarry's identity, its age, sex, and any other relevant information.

When the cast is dry, cut out the soil round the plaster and remove completely – Figure 63/5. Pull back the supporting card, wash off all mud and earth and pack carefully in newspaper for transit. If it is necessary to move it before it has set completely, leave any debris attached to it and remove it later. It can be hardened by baking it slowly. Take care however, not to apply too fierce a heat as the cast will be apt to crumble.

Be particularly careful to wash out the mixing container as soon as the mixture has been poured out on to the print, otherwise what is left will harden and be difficult to remove.

Before the plaster cast is quite set, a loop of string or wire can be inserted into it at the back so that the cast can subsequently be hung up. If casts are to be kept in good condition for any length of time they should be stored in a flat box.

What you have at the moment is a cast of a foot – figure 64/6 – which is very useful for making sign on the age stands (chapter 14).

To produce a replica of the sign gently press the cast into plasticine. This gives a clean impression of the sign.

To make a plaster cast representation of the original sign as a more permanent record than the plasticine, build a plasticine bund around the base of your original cast. Next paint the face of the cast with a soap solution. Mix up some more plaster and pour it into the bund. When the plaster has set you can gently try to prise the two casts apart, after removing the bund. If this proves too difficult you may have to break up the original cast in order to preserve the new positive cast.

The first cast you made, the negative, can be used as a tool with your age stand. By pressing the cast into your age stand or tracking lanes you can make an impression of the original sign. This can be observed to note the ageing process, allowing you to record the sign's deterioration over time. When you do this make sure that the weather conditions are favourable, that is, not too wet.

PART FOUR

The Future

CHAPTER TWENTY-FIVE

Developments in Tracking

This is the end of the book but not the finish of the story. This is the start of your tracking career. Whether you are involved with tracking as an adjunct to some other profession or as an art in itself, this book will have given you a good basis upon which to build.

Finally, I would like to indicate areas which in my opinion will become important in the medium term to people who are involved in tracking. I can see two main areas for future development, they are:

- Technical
- Personal

TECHNICAL

As with any other skill which can trace its ancestry back to ancient times, there is often resistance amongst its practitioners to keep abreast of the latest technological breakthroughs. There are, however, a few areas which I consider can be of great help to the modern sophisticated tracker.

Thermal imaging

The use of thermal imaging (TI) technology is well established in the military, the fire service, and with search and rescue organisations for seeing in obscured environments such as smoke or moonless nights. This application can be used by the tracker team, but TI can also be used to detect heat sources.

Applying the equipment to this effect will give the tracker two advantages:

- The tracker will be able to detect the presence of the quarry which is otherwise hidden from view
- The tracker will be able to give a better estimate as to the age of sign

Night vision goggles and infra red torches
The use of night vision goggles will enable the tracker to carry on tracking well beyond the normal hours permitted by nature, especially if they are augmented with infra red light sources. It must be appreciated that this equipment is not without its drawbacks. For instance, the peripheral vision of the wearer is severely restricted and with most designs the depth of field is very difficult to judge.

Information technology
It has been brought to the reader's attention how big a part intelligence and information gathering play in the tracker's role. Because of this emphasis it would be remiss of the modern tracker not to take advantage of all the efficient methods that are available today to transfer, collate and record this data.

Digital photography
This subject is in its infancy with respect to its application to tracking but, with the advent of digital cameras and digital video recorders, it would seem that there is an area ripe for development. Computers can be used to store, collate and compare as well as to enhance the imagery with 3D effects and by modifying the colour and tonal properties of a picture.

DNA tracking
A day doesn't seem to pass without a report in the newspapers about the latest application of DNA studies in the solving of crimes. To this end the modern tracker must be aware of the importance of preserving, gathering, recording, or marking the location of any material left by the quarry.

Global Positioning System (GPS)
South African game parks are now utilising the latest technology to keep records of their wildlife. With the aid of hand-held computers using a graphics display, trackers with poor or non-existent literacy skills can record the location of prints and animals. In this way the parks can use the vast amount of information which the trackers see but have been previously unable to record, to build up a picture of the movement patterns of the animals. It is a classic harnessing of modern technology and ancient skills to produce valuable results.

PERSONAL

As I commented in the Introduction, I hope that this study will enhance your knowledge and appreciation of your hobby or your profession. I'm sure that the outdoor pursuits teacher, the conservationist, the wildlife enthusiast will gain as much from this book as the military tracker because, as with all experts and dedicated people, they do not stop learning. Even if they have never considered tracking as being in their remit, they will see the benefits that can spin off from it into their sphere.

What is important is the recognition of personal development and to that end I suggest that you record any comments, observations, or experiences that relate to tracking. One can see one's development as a continual progression and, the more the earlier practices are applied, the more progress will be made.

The following will encourage and stimulate your personal development:

- Courses and structured training
- Discussion and feedback via the internet
- Practice and the critical analysis of the lessons learnt

Index